Return
Engagement

Return

Engagement

A Postscript to "Moscow Rehearsals"

By

Norris Houghton

Holt, Rinehart and Winston · New York

Preface

I know some people for whom one look at the Soviet Union
is enough. Confused by its paradoxes, dismayed by its standard
of living, angered by its intolerance, disgruntled by its red
tape, they cry "Never again!" as they cross its borders and find
themselves back in the familiar West.

I am not one of these. Of course, I, too, am confused by
the Russian paradoxes and annoyed by the Russian pro-
crastination and prevarication. But, since my moments of ex-
hilaration seem to outweigh the waves of depression, I have
always been honestly sorry to leave the country.

My first Moscow appearance, so to speak, was in 1934. Lest
the reader be misled by my figure of speech, let me hasten to
say that, although it is true the theatre is my field, I was there
not as a performer but as a spectator. I stayed from September
until February, 1935. Two years later I returned to Moscow
for a few weeks, and, during World War II, I was twice in the
Soviet Union on U.S. Navy missions, though neither time in
Moscow.

In 1960, I played my first real "return engagement" in
Moscow. This book is the result. Twenty-five years between
engagements is a long time. Inevitably, things have changed,

and it was to observe and record these changes that I went back. I, of course, have changed, too. And this complicates judgments. Does the theatre mean to me today what it meant to me then? Do I understand people and events better now than I did at that time? Have my accumulated experiences both in life and art during the intervening one-third of my expected life span made me more tolerant or more exacting, more cynical or more appreciative? I can only say that I have done my best to recognize these possible changes and to maintain a balanced point of view.

The subjects on which I am reporting, as a result of the three months of my return engagement, are the same ones to which I limited myself in the thirties: the life, the training, and the work of artists in the dramatic theatre. Cinema, opera, and especially the ballet occupy, as all the world knows, major positions among the Russian performing arts, but, since I have no more than a casual layman's knowledge and appreciation of these fields, they receive only casual mention in this book. Again, as in 1934–1935, I chose to spend almost my entire time in Moscow, which is the theatrical as well as political capital of the Soviet Union; consequently, my conclusions about the Russian theatre are based solely on the work in Moscow, which seems to me now, as earlier, to provide most of the inspiration and leadership for the flourishing, but tributary, stages in other parts of the country.

In 1960, I was able to allow myself approximately half as much time for on-the-spot observations as I was able to allow myself earlier; thus, it has been impossible to explore some of Moscow's theatres in this book in quite as great detail as I did in my first book, *Moscow Rehearsals*. Consequently, it has seemed appropriate to call this book a postscript rather than a sequel. In the unlikely event that a reader turns to this volume with my earlier *Moscow Rehearsals* freshly in mind, he may be struck by certain repetitions. These I justify on the grounds that the majority of my readers will not have had recent access to that ancient tome, now long out-of-print, and that they will therefore find helpful some brief background that automatically involves repetition of earlier material. Further, in many instances I justify reiterations of past observations on the grounds that a number of facts about the Russian theatre and its artists remain unchanged after a quarter of a century, and that, occasionally, it is this very reiteration wherein the significance lies.

There may be readers of this book who will disagree with my transliterations of Russian proper names. Such transliterations always pose difficult problems, but in general I have adhered to the system I employed in *Moscow Rehearsals,* which insofar as possible conforms to that recommended by the Slavonic Division of the New York Public Library.

Two or three acknowledgments are definitely in order: to the John Simon Guggenheim Memorial Foundation, for a fellowship which made possible a good portion of my trip; to the Institute for Advanced Studies in the Theatre Arts, through whose good offices I went to Moscow as a participant in the Cultural Exchange Program set up between the governments of the United States and the U.S.S.R.; to the Ministry of Culture of the U.S.S.R., which acted as a most courteous and coöperative host during my first six weeks in Moscow; and, finally, to the large number of Russian theatre folk whose welcome was warm and whose hospitality, as some of the ensuing pages will testify, was both generous and rewarding.

NORRIS HOUGHTON

Contents

Contents

Return
Engagement

1

The Theatre

Revisited

Curtain time in Moscow comes at seven-thirty. By seven o'clock crowds are milling about the city's twenty-five playhouses. To the throngs pressing through the doors are added dozens of people who stand outside on the sidewalk, hoping to pick up or get rid of a spare ticket. *"Bilyety?"* they inquire, hopefully. By seven-twenty, everyone fortunate enough to obtain a ticket is inside, for, once the lights go down, no one is seated, and it takes a good ten minutes to get through the queue at the cloakrooms, where everyone is required to check hat and coat and galoshes.

It was the autumn of 1960, and I had not been to a Moscow theatre for twenty-three years. I always find it exciting to mingle with a theatre audience and to share its eager expectancy, but this return to the Russian capital, after almost a quarter of a century, filled me with more than usual animation. Not only was I looking forward to what I would see on the stage, but I was also intensely curious to see the Rus-

sians themselves. Would they look as I remembered them?
Would they comport themselves at the theatre as they used
to comport themselves? Would they reveal what was on their
minds through their reactions to the drama on the stage?

Already, outside the playhouse, it was apparent from the
size of the crowd that the stage still retained its power to
attract. Inside, I looked about the auditorium. Every seat was
filled, as it was to be at least ninety per cent of the sixty or so
times I would attend a theatre in the ensuing weeks. In one
way, the audience seemed unchanged. There was the same
preponderance of young faces. A Broadway crowd tends to
look affluent and middle-aged, which is no wonder, since only
the affluent middle-aged can afford the prices. But the Moscow playgoer who purchases the best seat in the house finds
it has cost him twenty-five rubles, which, by the exchange
values of 1960, was no more than two-and-a-half dollars. Thus
it is no wonder that so many bright young faces peered over
the balcony rails to watch the rest of us come in. But, in other
ways, the audience looked quite different from the way I remembered it. Now it more closely resembled audiences
throughout the rest of the world, and this was almost disappointing! During the long intermissions, when everybody
either promenades counterclockwise in the huge foyers or else
seats himself in one of the theatre's several snack bars for a
cheese or a caviar sandwich—or a dish of ice cream, a soft
drink, or a beer—I caught no sight of babushkas wearing
shawls tightly over their heads, nor of youths with Russian
embroidered shirts buttoned sidewise under their chins and
with trousers stuffed into boots. Furthermore, there was only
a sprinkling of Red Army soldiers in baggy, olive drab uni-
forms. Now the men were dressed in dark, single- or double-
breasted business suits, white shirts, and neckties. Here and
there a shy, self-conscious youth even sported a black bow
tie with his black suit, in pathetic imitation of the evening

clothes he had seen in pictures of Capitalist origin. The women, though not really chic, were not badly dressed. They displayed more taste for bright colors and for rayon satin (and less taste for décolletage) than do our better-dressed women, and many of them wore lipstick. There was even some simple costume jewelry in evidence. Lipstick and jewelry—what a difference they made! Both were unheard of in the thirties. The Russians were beginning to look like the bourgeoisie.

In the course of the next several weeks, I discovered, to my amazement, that not only do today's Moscow audiences more closely resemble bourgeois audiences in appearance than they did in 1934–1935, but also that they now even react very much as do their Western counterparts. In the thirties, the Russian theatregoers had reminded me of spectators at a ball game, sitting on the edges of their seats, ready to cheer the plays and the players. Now they seemed more blasé. The stage, upon which they had gazed with wide-eyed amazement in the thirties, had come to be taken as a matter of course. Frequently, as I discovered, half of the audience was on its feet and headed for cloakrooms before the second curtain call.

Yet there were far more important changes to be observed in the Moscow theatre of 1960. These were obvious in the plays I saw. They were also obvious in the discussions I had with directors and actors and students whom I met during my visit. The Central Lecture Auditorium of the Polytechnical Museum is a famous spot where the Revolutionary poets, Alexander Blok and Vladimir Mayakovski, used to read their blood-tingling verses, and from whose podium Lenin is reputed to have addressed his awed followers. Toward the end of my visit, I was asked to lecture in this hall. Then again, young people dominated the audience of more than twelve hundred that jammed every bank of sternly unupholstered golden oak seats. They were students straight from classes and young white-collar workers carrying book satchels and briefcases. For the hour and a half that my lecture and its translation lasted, they were appreciatively attentive. Then came their turn: the question period. The written question is customary in Moscow, and no sooner had I paused for breath than the slips of paper on which questions were written began to descend toward the lectern, passed hand over hand. There were lined sheets torn from notebooks, scraps of lavender graph paper, a corner torn from a newspaper, a piece of tissue paper from heaven knows where—anything the audience could get its hands on. When all the unsigned slips were assembled, there were seventy-five of them, some containing two or three questions. Manfully, I started at the top of the pile. But I had disposed of only the first dozen or so when the time came to yield the hall to the next event, so I swept up the unanswered questions and stuffed them into my pocket.

Later that night, back at the National Hotel, I pored over these questions. Some were neatly penned in careful English, some scrawled in nearly undecipherable Russian. The ones that interested me most were those that revealed an almost unbelievable knowledge of the American theatre. I say unbelievable because, lacking access to Western newspapers, periodicals, and books, whence came the background for such questions as: "Does Eva Le Gallienne still take part in the work of your Phoenix Theatre?" (She had played *Mary Stuart* there three years earlier, but I had not mentioned this fact in my lecture.) "Some words, please, about *Raisin in the Sun.*" "Tell us about the latest performances of the plays of Beckett and Ionesco in New York." (Neither author has ever been published or performed in the U.S.S.R.) "What is the impact on off-Broadway of the present-day beatnik trend?"

Toward the bottom of the pack lay the one really remarkable slip. On the outside was written in English, "To the Lecturer *Directly*." Inside, also in English, I read:

We would like very much to know several things concerning not American but Soviet theatre as you see it NOW.

1. What do you think has caused gross deterioration of the Soviet theatre?

2. Whom [sic] of Soviet producers do you believe to be really gifted and able today?

3. What is your opinion of the future of our theatre?

I am not altogether sorry this slip of paper lay toward the bottom. It would have been tricky to deal with on the spur of the moment. Was it a loaded question designed to unmask my true (and supposedly alien) sentiments? Did it actually reflect the interrogator's disenchantment with his own theatre? Assuming the question was not loaded, how much weight should have been accorded to the point of view of this one questioner out of seventy-five? I wish I could have met him. I wish we could have discussed the many paradoxes I was encountering on every hand; could have argued about who was and who was not "really gifted and able" in the Russian theatre today, by comparison with a quarter of a century ago. That quarter century had begun to seem a very long period of time.

The year 1935 had been a year of titans. In that year Constantin Stanislavski and Vladimir Nemirovich-Danchenko, both white-haired and leonine, still stood erect at the helm of the Moscow Art Theatre, having guided it for almost forty years through the hurricane of Revolution. True, one of these, Stanislavski, was ailing and thus seldom went to his theatre; but he conducted rehearsals at home, worked feverishly on his books, and labored to train a younger generation of directors to succeed himself, and a younger generation of actors to follow Ivan Moskvin, Vasily Kachalov, and Olga Knipper-Chekhova, actors whose abilities had been combined with his own talents and those of Nemirovich to make the Moscow Art Theatre one of the greatest ensembles in the world.

In that year, also, there had been Vsevolod Meierhold. In a shabby playhouse on what is now Gorki Street, Meierhold, who was the stormy petrel of the Revolutionary theatre and its most original genius (and who rather looked like some sea bird, with his sharp beak of a nose and his thin, gray wind-swept forelock), had barked at and cajoled his actors, concoct-ing out of them his special brand of theatre magic. It had, in fact, been a magic so special that it—and he—were soon to be done away with, branded as enemies of the Revolution. Yet, in 1935, Meierhold was still poring over the plans for a theatre which he was never to see built, and talking brilliantly, like Treplev in *The Sea Gull,* about the need for new forms, all the while paying no heed to the storm clouds that were build-ing up behind him.

Out on Tverskoi Boulevard, in 1935, Alexander Tairov already had a fine new streamlined building in which to house his Kamerny Theatre. A round-faced, balding little man, he was famous throughout Western Europe for his productions of *Giroflé-Girofla, Desire Under the Elms, Phèdre,* and *Saint Joan,* though in a very short time he, too, was to go.

True, Eugene Vakhtangov was already dead by the thirties. But, in 1935, his colleagues and disciples, working in the theatre that bore his name, inspired one with their collective fervor, so that although there was no single titan among them, they stood as a group worthy of challenging each of the older greats.

There was, too, in 1935, a dynamic younger generation. I remember young Nikolai Okhlopkov, blond and lanky and

looking remarkably like Charles A. Lindbergh. Okhlopkov
had a hall out in the workingman's district of Krasnaya
Presnaya, and there he was pioneering in the use of arena-
style staging long before anyone in America (save perhaps
Glenn Hughes and his pupils in Seattle) had heard of such
a thing. Fired by Meierhold's call for a "theatre theatrical"
in opposition to the realistic style of the Moscow Art Theatre,
Okhlopkov had not only thrown out the proscenium but was
introducing elements from the Chinese theatre and from
commedia dell'arte.

Then, too, among the younger generation there was
Natalia Sats, the slender, chic daughter of an eminent composer. Natalia Sats had organized one of the first, if not *the*
first, of the children's theatres in the U.S.S.R., and was therefore the pioneer in a movement which was to grow until it
had no parallel in any country. In a very few years she was to
drop out of sight and the theatre she started was to fall into
other hands, her own name obliterated.

Stanislavski, Nemirovich-Danchenko, Meierhold, Tairov,
Vakhtangov, Okhlopkov, and Natalia Sats—these were the
artists who had given their stamp to one or another Soviet
theatre during the years from 1917 to 1937. In Moscow there
is not, and there has not been for forty years, any such free-
lance creativity as underpins all Broadway and London's
West End; work in Moscow takes place within the continuity
of a permanent theatre company which becomes the member
artist's home, perhaps for a decade, perhaps for a lifetime.
Each of the great directors had his own building, whose very
architectural features were dictated by the director's individual vision of theatre; each had his own sub-directors and designers, who assisted in carrying out his creative ideas; and,
most important of all, each director had a company of actors
with whom he worked on play after play, so that the actors all
came to speak the same artistic language. Together, each

company, under its own direction, developed its individual approach to the theatre.

Thus, each theatre bore a different stylistic stamp. On what might be called the conservative side stood the Moscow Art Theatre—"conservative" because it upheld the basic tradition of the Russian theatre, a tradition which was codified by Stanislavski before the Revolution and which was, in its literature and in its performance, essentially realistic. The Moscow Art Theatre was, in fact, the arch-exponent of realism. On the opposite, or radical, side stood Meierhold, who defied everything for which realism stood, who called such realism the expression of the nineteenth-century bourgeoisie—untheatrical, and unimaginative—and who demanded a return to the age-old concepts on which the Oriental theatre, the theatre of the Greeks, and the commedia dell'arte had been founded. It was between the Moscow Art Theatre and the Meierhold Theatre that the others were grouped—Vakhtangov, Tairov, Okhlopkov, and their followers, who acknowledged the greatness of both Stanislavski and Meierhold and sought to combine the best features of each in some new synthesis of outward form and inner truth.

What exactly was the realism of the Moscow Art Theatre? It is important to remember that it was never simply an external realism. Great attention was indeed paid to the sound of crickets and to the angle of the setting sun, to the historical accuracy of both cloak and dagger, to the "natural" movement and intonation of the actor. But these were only the outward appurtenances. The main thing to be achieved was psychological truth, and the appurtenances existed only to surround that truth with an environment that would nourish credibility. In Russian, the words of the title of Stanislavski's great statement of his system, published in English as *An Actor Prepares,* mean literally "The Work of the Actor on Himself." Thus the principal aim of the

Moscow Art Theatre lay in revealing to the actor the sources of his creativity, so that he could discern the psychological truth of the character he was to portray, make it his own, and then translate it into artistic truth. This was the key to an understanding of the Art Theatre. To analyze "the Method," which is what Stanislavski's system has come to be called in its American adaptation, would require a whole book alone (it took its creator two books and part of a third to expound it); but the important thing is that when I went to the Moscow Art Theatre in the thirties to see a performance of *The Cherry Orchard* or *The Lower Depths,* or of even such an authentically stylistic piece as Beaumarchais' *The Marriage of Figaro,* I did indeed feel a special freshness, as though what I witnessed were happening for the first time. I forgot I was in a theatre, for the actors seemed actually *to be* the people whom they were portraying, not just actors *pretending* to be them, and it seemed that I was actually being allowed to peer into their real lives. Their pains and their joys seemed not to be simulated but actual, and, because of the remarkable amalgam that is theatre at its best, I suffered and rejoiced with them, was carried out of myself, and became at one with them. The acting at the Art Theatre in those days was unsurpassed: There was Vasily Kachalov, in whose hands a pencil could assume almost independent life when he played with it as the Narrator in *Resurrection;* there was Ivan Moskvin, whose cracking voice and wide-eyed confusions made Yepikhodov in *The Cherry Orchard* an hilarious bumbler; Mikhail Tarkhanov, who spoke with the soft voice of all humanity when, as Luka, the pilgrim, he comforted a dying woman in *The Lower Depths;* Olga Knipper-Chekhova, Leonid Leonidov, Alexander Vishnevski, Nikolai Podgorny, all of them playing as a perfectly orchestrated ensemble.

At the Meierhold Theatre, the technique was in direct opposition to that of the Art Theatre. I was not asked to forget that I was in a theatre. I was not expected to believe that these characters were real people. As the actors raced and tumbled or paused and grimaced, I was constantly reminded that this was theatre, not life: Their make-up was exaggerated; their costumes were always costumes, not clothes; and they frequently addressed the audience directly. Everything about the performance—the auditorium that faced a proscenium barren of curtain, down whose aisles performers might unexpectedly charge; the stage without any reassuringly familiar setting of walls and ceiling, doors and windows, but only abstract forms or bare constructions; the musical accompaniment; the sharp beams of light from unconcealed sources that utilized color arbitrarily—everything was unreal, intensely theatrical. It is a subtle and tricky thing to evoke an audience's sympathy under these circumstances, for a different kind of relationship is established between performer and spectator. The relationship is a self-conscious one. It is the kind that Sophocles apparently achieved in his theatre, despite the masks his actors wore and despite a chorus which executed stylized movements as they chanted in verse.

In between these extreme positions, in 1935, stood the other theatres of the Moscow of that day.

At the Vakhtangov Theatre, the scenic environment was recognizable for what it was supposed to be—a room or a forest or a street. But it was usually recognizable only by a minimum of realistic detail, set against darkness or against a lighted cyclorama. The rest was left to the imagination. The performance had an underpinning of believability, but the actors seemed simultaneously to be impersonating the characters and yet, at the same time, making a comment on them. If this is hard to comprehend, try to recall a performance by Alfred Lunt and Lynn Fontanne. They have always struck me as being disciples of Vakhtangov without knowing it. Miss Fontanne and Mr. Lunt are always making you believe in the characters they are playing, but they are also always adding something of themselves, so that you are aware of their opinion of the characters. As Miss Fontanne plays with Mr. Lunt, they both seem to be saying to you: "Isn't this make-believe we're indulging in—and all of us know that's all that it *is*—great fun?"

At Okhlopkov's so-called Realistic Theatre in Krasnaya Presnaya, the synthesis of outer form and inner truth found still different expressions. There, the lack of any proscenium or of even a permanent stage platform brought spectators and performers into a physical proximity even closer than at the Meierhold. The shape of the arena was rarely the same: Sometimes action took place on platforms stretching in an L-shape along two walls of the rectangular hall, with movable seats for the public filling in the remaining space; at other times, two tangential platforms were placed diagonally across the hall; or there was a central lozenge, with the audience in the four corners; or, in one famous production, the action took place on bridges over the audience's heads. In those days, Okhlopkov's principal preoccupation seemed to be with the problem of space. Actually, however, he was experimenting with space only as a means to the solution of another problem: how to eliminate the psychological barrier he felt the old combination of footlights, orchestra pit, and curtained proscenium set up between the actors and their audience. He wanted to attain an almost physical participation on the part of the spectator in the sweep of the action, not the alienation that Meierhold often seemed to be seeking. In plays like Maxim Gorki's *Mother,* Alexander Serafimovich's *The Iron Flood,* and Nikolai Pogodin's *Aristocrats,* Okhlopkov brilliantly created this sense of "communion" (which was the word he liked to use), though one wondered whether these might not be tours de force and where he would go from there.

In addition, there was also Tairov's Kamerny Theatre, whose productions, such as that of Oscar Wilde's *Salome,* may have been hailed in the West partly because they were rather like the Western avant-garde's expressions of the twenties, with cubistic scenery and costumes, half-chanted speech, and semi-choreographed movement. Sounding like Jean Cocteau and his demand for "pure theatre," Tairov cried (in direct opposition to Stanislavski), "There are two truths: the truth of life and the truth of art." There were also some twenty-five other theatres in Moscow, led by the Maly, the oldest dramatic theatre in the city and the most beautifully housed, on Sverdlov Square at the shoulder of the Bolshoi. The Maly was the citadel of Alexander Ostrovski, the father of nineteenth-century Russian realism. There were the State Jewish Theatre, led by the great Yiddish-language actor, Solomon Mikhoels (and when I use the word "theatre," I mean a permanent acting company under a permanent leader occupying a permanent home); the State Gypsy Theatre; the Second Moscow Art Theatre, facing the Maly across Sverdlov Square; and the studio stages of Yuri Zavadski and Reuben Simonov, that rather resembled today's off-Broadway theatres in New York. And there were the Theatre of the Red Army and the theatres of the various trade unions which, in utility fashion, were known by such initials as MOSPS and VTSPS.

Here, in barest outline, was the Moscow theatre world of the mid-1930's. In my memory, it is now composed of fleeting, jostling glimpses: of Stanislavski holding out both hands as he greeted me in his book-and-sketch-lined study in the lamp-lit dusk of a late October afternoon; of Meierhold pouring a tumblerful of water over his head at a rehearsal of *The Marriage Proposal,* a piece of business he had just invented; of a stormy session of the Artistic Council of the Vakhtangov Theatre, presided over by Zakhava, which I was allowed to witness, as they discussed a run-through of a new play, *The Hat,* a drama they all knew to be of inferior quality; of my first night at the Realistic Theatre, when an actor on his entrance thrust a loaf of bread and a knife into the hands of the startled spectator sitting next to me and asked her to cut a slice for him while he went on with the business at hand; of the cheering audience at the Art Theatre pressing down to the footlights at the curtain calls for a closer glimpse of Kachalov, Moskvin, Knipper-Chekhova, and other faces now no longer visible.

The sixty or so performances I attended in Moscow's theatres during the fall of 1960 persuaded me that, although there are today no giants of the stature of Stanislavski, nor of Nemirovich-Danchenko, Meierhold, Tairov, or Vakhtangov, there is nonetheless vitality and variety, as well as hope and excitement, and that the people of the Moscow theatre are once again creating. True, most of my friends who were in Moscow between 1937 and 1957 had beheld a barren spectacle. Indeed, every Russian of authority in the theatre with whom I spoke confirmed this fact. During the better part of those two decades, the Communist Party under Stalin had forced the Soviet theatre into a conforming line of "socialist realism," even as I sensed in 1937 that it was about to do. Men like Meierhold, who fought for the maintenance of independence in creative expression, were either banished or executed. Fear seized the less spiritually hardy; a pall of sameness descended; experiments with what the Party line called "formalism" ceased. For almost twenty years, in effect, the Soviet stage stood still.

Then, in 1953, as everyone knows, the death of Stalin signaled a change in the intellectual climate. The long pent-up ferment of creative feeling boiled over violently, so violently, in fact, that the Party found it necessary to clamp

the lid down again in 1954—but not before Ilya Ehrenburg
had come out with his famous statement preceding his novel
The Thaw. "An author is not a piece of machinery register-
ing events," Ehrenburg wrote in the magazine *Znamya.* "An
author writes a book, not because he knows how to write, not
because he is a member of the Union of Soviet Writers and
may be asked why he has published nothing for so long. An
author does not write a book because he has to earn a living.
An author writes a book because he finds it necessary to tell
people something of himself, because he is pregnant with his
book, because he has seen people, things, and emotions that
he cannot help describing. . . . Can one imagine Tolstoi
being given an instruction to write *Anna Karenina* or Gorki
being ordered to write *Mother?*"

   This declaration of independence turned out to be somewhat premature, but it was an accurate expression for all but
the most reactionary Stalinist artists. In 1956, after Khrushchev had overturned the Communist apple cart with his
denigration of Stalin's image and of the "cult of personality,"
a second wave of freedom in the arts was set in motion. "The
sign had been given," as Edward Crankshaw has said, "for the
Soviet people, the writers above all, to share in the task of
setting the Soviet house in order." Yet this second wave then
also got out of hand, and it took Khrushchev himself, at the
remarkable garden party he gave for the writers of Moscow
in May, 1957, to warn his guests that the Party still had the
last word and that force would be used to bring them to heel
if, in its view, they expressed themselves too irresponsibly,
which was to say, too humanistically and personally. But,
despite the shock of Khrushchev's warning (one writer, it is
rumored, fainted dead away), things would never be quite the
same as they had been under Stalin. Russian writers today feel
confident. Mr. Crankshaw affirms (and I agree), that "the
Terror has gone forever, and that slowly, all too slowly, but

still surely, and in the teeth of bitter resistance from the en-
trenched 'reactionaries,' their country is moving into better
days."

In the theatre, too, these waves swept in and out and in
again. While the term "socialist realism" was not abrogated,
the word went out that it could be interpreted with as much
latitude as each creative artist might possess. "Today," say
Moscow's theatrical leaders, "we once again can breathe. We
can stir the embers that lie smoldering under the ash heap.
We can replace the gray sameness with the brightness we
recall from our youthful days in the theatre." But twenty
years is a long time, and the embers were almost cold. Four
years is barely time to catch up, and, in 1960, Moscow stages
were just beginning to provide an excitement comparable to
that of the early thirties. The tragedy is, of course, that during
those twenty years the rest of the world learned the lessons
which the Soviet theatre had taught in its great days, and
that it moved on while the Russians stood still. Brecht and
Piscator had, for example, learned from Meierhold, and the
rest of us had learned from Brecht. Consequently, what
seemed electrifying and revolutionary in 1935 has today become common coinage throughout the rest of the world, and
the Russians, who squelched their torches and stamped out
their own theatrical revolution for the sake of their political
one, still frequently find themselves (although most of them
are not fully aware of it) behind the rest of us. Now, in order
to recover their former preëminent position, actors and
directors are once more seeking new styles of performance
and adapting the traditions they have inherited to the new
Soviet day; and designers and technicians are demanding new
consideration.

2

First

Nights

On my first night in Moscow in 1960, I went to the Central Puppet Theatre of Sergei Obraztsov. Since it was early September, the company was still playing in its makeshift summer quarters in the Hermitage Gardens and not at its own charming, compact three-hundred-and-fifty-seat theatre on Gorki Street. But the location made no difference, for this would have been an evening of delight anywhere. The program was called *An Unusual Concert,* though, in a sense, it was not unusual at all: It contained the familiar ingredients of all concerts and variety programs rolled into one—and then rolled out again with such delicious mockery that you doubted whether you could ever again see with equanimity a patronizing, self-esteeming master of ceremonies (as well as master of the cliché), or a chorus of eager folk singers, or a breast-heaving prima donna, a Gypsy choir, a mike-hugging blues singer, a pompous German lieder singer, or a shaggy-haired cellist. The puppets are the kind that are operated from beneath the stage, and the company of almost forty puppeteers, trained by Sergei Obraztsov, accomplished miracles. No telltale shudder of a shoulder, no lowering of an eyelid was overlooked by the all-knowing dolls. The theatre has a marvelous knack for portraying puppet animals, too; and *An Unusual Concert* happily included performing dogs as well as divas, a hen and a spaniel who did a duet, and, as an unlikely but rewarding spectacle, a cageful of lions who took turns riding around a circus ring on horseback.

This first evening was a happy reminder that the Russians and I could still laugh at the same things. But it was the next night that provided a more significant clue to the improving state of the Russian theatre, for on that second night I went to a dramatic theatre, the Mossoviet, to see Yuri Zavadski's production of *The Merry Wives of Windsor*. The Mossoviet is housed in one of the newest playhouses in Moscow. The building was completed in 1958, and its fluorescent-lighted auditorium, consisting of an orchestra floor and three galleries, seats twelve hundred people. The orchestra is so steeply raked that the back row is about half as far from the stage as the back row of a house of comparable capacity in New York's West Forties. Like most Moscow theatres, there is a good-sized orchestra pit between front row and footlights, which can be partially or completely covered as the production scheme dictates. There are runways from the sides of the stage forward to proscenium doors, so that entrances can be made in front of the curtain line. Steps descend from the apron to the center aisle for ingress and egress through the audience.

All these facilities were utilized to the full in this Shakespearean evening. It was a boisterous, good-humored performance. A score by Khachaturian enhanced the roistering mood. The Falstaff was good (although not the best I had ever seen), and the Mistresses Page and Ford came off as a fine couple of wenches. Mistress Quickly, looking rather like Mrs. Wiggs of the Cabbage Patch, kept up a running fire of gags directed at the audience; and, though these asides had little to do with the Bard, they delighted the spectators.

There were also some rather extraneous figures in long-nosed commedia dell'arte masks and bright patchwork dominoes who wandered in and out trying to be helpful, and there was one even more extraneous man in modern evening dress. If they served no other end, at least the former prepared the audience for a bit of Italian sixteenth-century street carnival, which took place in the lobby during the second intermission. As the audience came out of the auditorium at that point, they found their usual promenade space filled with booths. Barkers and tricksters shouted for attention. Pandemonium held sway for twenty minutes; then the harlequin figures swiftly folded their tents and scampered away, and the public filed back to their seats for the last act.

I must admit that there seemed to be a good deal of confusion, both of style and intent, in this production. Its significance for me was that it was fresh and exuberant, unencumbered by grim realism, and that it was free to wander where and as it pleased, with no social message apparent (the man in evening dress, for example, was expatiating rather more on Elizabethan England than on communism). Yet two characteristics of Soviet performance were noticeable that evening, characteristics which in time come to be taken for granted, but which regularly interest the newly arrived visitor from Broadway. These characteristics are: first, overacting; and second, slowness of pace. Certainly the Russians have a florid style of performance. It is a style which is thrown into sharp relief by our own comparative reticence of statement. The Russians seem to rant and gesticulate to excess. If they were to be told that this apparent overacting reduces the credibility of their productions for us, the Russians would be

incredulous. Thus I am led to the conclusion that what
appears excessive alongside our contained expression is
actually only the natural Russian exuberance that regularly
manifests itself even offstage by more emphatic gestures and
tones than we customarily employ. The arm-waving and fore-
finger-pointing of street-corner disputants; the shouts on a
crowded Moscow trolley-bus, as passengers elbow each other
toward the exit; as well as the table-thumping and shoe-wav-
ing of contemporary Soviet diplomacy are all signs of this
same difference. Such things seem less abnormal to the Russians than they do to those of us who have been bred in an
Anglo-Saxon world of understatement and controlled emotion. Generally, the Slav believes feelings should be expressed;
the American believes there is a virtue in concealing them.
There is no right or wrong here, only a divergence of temperament and custom.

The pace of Russian acting, or rather the lack of pace, may
reflect a temperamental difference, too. Speed is an American
virtue which is not so valued throughout the rest of the world.
Just as the tempo of New York daily life leaves the foreign
visitor breathless, so does our theatre's tempo of performance.
Conversely, the leisure of a Russian spectacle calls forth
American impatience. "Why don't they get on with the
show?" we frequently ask. In Russia, the curtain of *Death of
a Salesman* rises at seven-thirty and finally falls at a quarter to
twelve. Without the addition of a single line or of a single
intermission, its playing time has been increased by a good
hour and a quarter. *A Memory of Two Mondays*, which
Arthur Miller wrote as a curtain raiser to *A View from the
Bridge* and which he intended to play for an hour or so, lasts
in its Russian presentation for three hours. Whereas this slow
pace may be useful in drawing both performers and spectators
deeper into the inner life of a Chekhov play than is our fast-
motion treatment, it vitiates the impact of such works as those

of Miller, which were intended for our hard-hitting, rapid-fire, hammer-blow theatre. But the Russians justify their slow pace by asserting that it is rhythm, not tempo, which they seek; and, they say, rhythm comes from the nature of the material, which, in turn, derives from life. A George Abbott speed, when arbitrarily imposed for stylistic reasons on the normal tempo of life, is as inexplicable to the Russian viewer of our stage as their slow-motion technique is to us.

One of the surprises and delights for the New Yorker who visits Moscow is the richness of classical fare available. Take, for instance, the two consecutive evenings I spent at the Maly Theatre, first at an adaptation of Thackeray's *Vanity Fair* and then at Tolstoi's *The Living Corpse.*

In *Vanity Fair,* a narrator (that perennial prop of novel adapters) is the first to appear onstage. He is garbed as a circus ringmaster, complete with top hat, white riding breeches, and whip. Behind him, the stage is hung with a gaily painted curtain depicting period scenes of London and of English country life. Suddenly this whole curtain begins to revolve merry-go-round fashion away from the audience; revolving with it, the principal characters go riding by on merry-go-round figures, each in the frozen attitude of a caricature, the ringmaster introducing them to us one by one. When the circle has come full swing, the section of the cylindrical curtain that now faces the audience opens on the first scene: Becky Sharp's arrival at the Sedleys'. She is a bouncing Becky, really only a trifle too old for the early scenes. When this episode comes to an end, the curtain closes, begins to revolve sidewise again for a little, then halts. Another sections opens. This occurs thirteen times during the course of the production.

The most memorable scenes of the performance were those in Miss Crawley's sitting room, for Miss Crawley was played that night by the senior actress of the Soviet Union, ninety-three-year-old Alexandra Yablochkina. When the double doors parted and she was rolled on in her wheel chair, the audience, on almost the only occasion during my Moscow theatregoing, interrupted the scene with a spontaneous wave of affectionate applause that rocked the chandelier. I was seated in a stage box and so could see the grand old lady clearly. She, who had been a fifty-year-old leading actress of the Maly at the time of the Revolution in 1917, deserved, if anyone ever did, her title of People's Artist of the U.S.S.R., for she has served her public faithfully for three-quarters of a century. That night her smile was warm, her eyes bright, her hand firm as she picked up her teacup; and she seemed blessedly spared that infirmity of old actors, a failing memory, for every line came through on cue and unfalteringly. At one point, as though to reassure the audience that she could do so, she rose from her wheel chair and moved rather spryly about the room. When she made her final exit, a second loving ovation brought tears to Muscovite and Manhattan eyes alike. We Americans neglect and discard our stage favorites too soon, I said to myself, as I watched the door close on her retreating figure.

The dark anguish of Tolstoi's *The Living Corpse* contrasted deeply with the generally bright image of *Vanity Fair*. This page from nineteenth-century Russia was illuminated by acting which bore a strong resemblance to the Moscow Art Theatre in its heyday. It was as though the clock had been turned back and we were again living in Tolstoi's time. Every detail of great country-house life was laid out before us: latticed pavilions that afforded views across golden fields to the horizon; lofty drawing rooms with furniture and chandeliers swathed in white linen dust covers; jowly old butlers and lithe young footmen; neighbors and house-party guests; dowagers in long, cream-colored lace gowns and

hothouse beauties carrying parasols to protect their com-
plexions.

St. Petersburg salons were recreated with equal care: little
silk damask-walled morning rooms where elderly ladies sipped
chocolate *à la française* and gossiped *comme tout le monde;*
gilt-paneled reception rooms where dandies, wearing side-
burns and boutonnieres, vied for the attentions of taffeta-
gowned debutantes. The sordid was, naturally, also revealed:
a gaslit back room in a house of ill-repute, with its vulgar
orange-and-green wallpaper, where drunken young guard
officers held peroxide blondes on their laps and listened to the
music of Gypsies, whose proud eyes seemed fixed on some
other image far away; the dreary saloon where Fedya re-
counted his amazing story over cheap liquor; the bleak
provincial courtroom, with its green-black frock-coated attendants wearing pince-nez, where the tragic denouement
unfolded.

I never saw Fedya played by the great Austrian actor,
Alexander Moissi, nor by John Barrymore, nor by Stanislavski
himself, but the performance by Mikhail Tsaryov, of the tor-
tured aristocrat who gives up his wife to her lover by pretending that he himself is dead, was masterful. There are,
incidentally, forty-six speaking parts in the play, plus a
Gypsy chorus of twenty, plus innumerable extras, so that it
would be safe to say the Maly production employs approximately seventy-five performers. No wonder we seldom see the
play performed in the West! Tsaryov himself, incidentally,
is the Artistic Director of the Maly. Quite unlike our theatre
directors, many of the principal *régisseurs* of Moscow's companies still are or once were important actors. On occasion,
I have seen Reuben Simonov, the Artistic Director of the
Vakhtangov, play in his theatre the leading male role in
Filumena Marturano by Eduardo de Filippo; Mikhail
Kedrov, the Artistic Director of the Moscow Art Theatre,

appear there in Gogol's *Dead Souls;* Tsaryov act again in
Chekhov's *Ivanov* on his own Maly stage; and Oleg Yefremov
play a character role in Rozov's *The Immortal Ones* at the
Sovremennik Theatre, of which he is the Artistic Director.
And I have seen Nikolai Okhlopkov himself perform in
many films. Not one of our major American *régisseurs* performs today. Of course, there is a precedent for such a custom
in Moscow, for Stanislavski himself acted for many years on
the stage of his own theatre.

Although I went almost nightly to the theatre during my
stay in Moscow, I saw but a fraction of the productions on
view. In fact, if I had been physically able to do so, in the
Soviet capital I might have attended, between the sixteenth
and the thirty-first of October, one hundred and fifty-eight
performances of straight plays; forty-five performances of
opera, operetta, and ballet; and thirty-three performances in
Moscow's puppet, children's, and young people's theatres. I
know of nowhere in the world where two hundred and thirty-
six different theatrical productions are offered in the space
of sixteen days.

In addition to these two hundred and thirty-six productions, all of which were, of course, professional ones, a number of semiprofessional performances were also taking place
during the same period in Moscow. These performances were
in the so-called People's Theatres, whose personnel come from
the city's factories and schools and other institutions in much
the manner of our own community theatres. But it is the professional theatre which is our principal concern, and also the
amazing fact that a total of one hundred and fifty-eight performances of dramatic works (as opposed to operas, ballets,
etc.) took place during sixteen days in October, 1960.

This huge total is the result of the repertory system, about
which there is so much loose talk and so little action in

America. There are twenty-five theatrical companies in Moscow, three of which—the Maly, the Moscow Art Theatre, and the Central Theatre of the Soviet Army—have two playhouses apiece: a main stage and a so-called "Filial" stage. And each of these companies has from eight or ten (at the smaller theatres) to twenty-eight plays (at the Art Theatre) which it is prepared to offer in the course of a season. Each theatre changes its bill nightly, the companies with two stages offering a different play on each stage every evening. For example, during that last half of October the Art Theatre presented:

On the main stage: *

Oct. 16 (mat.)   *The Blue Bird* (Maeterlinck)
     16 (eve.)   *The Third Pathetique* (Pogodin)
     18, 21, 28   *Maria Stuart* (Schiller)
     19   *The Three Sisters* (Chekhov)
     20, 26   *A Winter's Tale* (Shakespeare)
     22   *Dead Souls* (Gogol)
     23 (mat.)   *The Blue Bird* (Maeterlinck)
     23 (eve.)   *The Third Pathetique* (Pogodin)
     24, 27   *The Brothers Karamazov* (Dostoyevski)
     25   *The Sea Gull* (Chekhov)
     29   *The Golden Carriage* (Leonov)
     30 (mat.)   *The Blue Bird* (Maeterlinck)
     30 (eve.)   *Battle Along the Road* (Nikolaev)

At the Filial:

Oct. 16 (mat.)   *The Cherry Orchard* (Chekhov)
     16 (eve.)   *The Smug Citizens* (Gorki)
     18, 24, 27   *Death of a Salesman* (Miller)
     19   *The Road Through Sokolniki* (Razdolski)

* On October 17 and 31, the main stage was occupied by the Maly Company. On October 18 and 25 the Art Theatre presented, on the Maly's stage, Figueiredo's *The Fox and the Grapes* and Shaw's *The Devil's Disciple*. This exchange system allows each company one day off a week.

20, 26		*Jupiter Laughs* (Cronin)
21, 29		*A Doll's House* (Ibsen)
22		*The Autumn Garden* (Hellman)
23	(mat.)	*A Nest of Gentlefolk* (Turgenev)
23	(eve.)	*Uncle Vanya* (Chekhov)
25		*The Fox and the Grapes* (Figueiredo)
28		*A Nest of Gentlefolk* (Turgenev)
30	(mat.)	*A Nest of Gentlefolk* (Turgenev)
30	(eve.)	*Everything Belongs to the People* (Aleshin)

To produce on the scale of the Art Theatre requires a huge acting company. It is therefore less surprising than it might be to learn that the roster of the Mosow Art Theatre today numbers one hundred and forty performers. Some of the senior members may not play more than ten or twelve times a month; none of the company, I think it safe to say, plays the eight performances a week that are required of a Broadway actor. But then, probably two or three plays (and in the case of major theatres twice that number) are in rehearsal at the same time, and since almost every actor is involved in one or another of them, the average actor's schedule is full.

The schedule of the Art Theatre's presentations during this typical fortnight not only indicates the composition of the repertoire of Moscow's most distinguished company, but it also indicates the relative popularity of its various productions, judged by the number of times a work has been repeated during this particular fortnight. All sorts of logistics, of course, also enter into the scheduling; furthermore, the plays that have been performed for decades, such as *Dead Souls* or *The Cherry Orchard,* are naturally played less frequently than are the newer additions to the repertoire. Certainly, the most striking fact about this fortnight's presentations is the preponderance of classics (twelve) over new works (nine), plus the fact that only five Soviet plays were performed.

Any theatre that can mount performances of twenty-one different plays in sixteen days deserves the respectful, indeed the awed, salute of all stage workers everywhere. This is what a repertory theatre in action should truly be. Not all these productions, of course, are new ones of the 1960 season. Many of them, such as *Dead Souls,* have been in the repertoire for twenty-five years or longer; others, such as the Chekhov plays, have been performed for almost sixty years. On the other hand, a new production of *A Doll's House* was added last season, as was a new production of *A Winter's Tale* the season before. If one went to every play presented at the Art Theatre (or any other theatre for that matter), one could thus probably see a cross section of its best work stretching back to its very beginnings.

3

Plays and

Playwrights Today

Shakespeare, Thackeray, Tolstoi. I have described the performances of works by these playwrights in order to introduce the reader to present-day Russian actors, directors, theatres, and styles of performance. But the lifeblood of the contemporary stage is not, or should not be, Shakespeare, nor Thackeray, nor Tolstoi. Neither should it be the Art Theatre's revivals of Maeterlinck, nor of Schiller, nor of Chekhov and the others that make up most of its repertoire. Rather it must be the plays and playwrights of today.

The smash hit of Moscow in the 1960–1961 season was *An Irkutsk Story*, a contemporary play by Alexei Arbuzov. Like all popular dramas in Russia, both classical and contemporary, it was simultaneously in the repertoires of a number of theatres in Moscow, as well as throughout the country; and one can thus, by comparing some of these different performances, learn a great deal not only about the play itself but also about the ways in which the various theatres differ in style and in production techniques.

At the Vakhtangov Theatre, *An Irkutsk Story* was given a performance which I would have recognized anywhere as a product of that company. All the earmarks were there: music to heighten the emotional impact of a scene, including bits of a lullaby or a folk song played on an accordion or a guitar, or a haunting theme played on a far-away solo violin; and simple, suggestive scenery which, in this case, consisted principally of a long, steep ramp that stretched upward and away from the footlights toward the rear of the stage. Down this path, toward the footlights, shoulder-to-shoulder as the curtain rose, entered the principal characters, workers on a hydroelectric project in Irkutsk, the misty impression of which was projected by light against the backdrop. At the foot of the ramp these characters were met by four men who were dressed uniformly in navy blue double-breasted suits, a sort of quartet of Thornton Wilder Stage Managers who served as the Chorus. Thus the performance began.

The plot of *An Irkutsk Story* may seem like soap opera by American standards. There is a girl named Valya, and there are two boys, Victor and Sergei, who are both in love with her. She marries Sergei, and the two live happily. Valya gives birth to twins. Then Sergei is drowned saving the lives of two neighbor children. The remainder of the play deals with the matured Victor's effort, which is finally successful, to persuade Valya to sublimate her personal tragedy in a life of work. The play is an only slightly vulgarized Communist *Our Town*. Its Chorus does for its slender story what Wilder's Stage Manager does for his: It extends the frame of reference and provides an almost pantheistic lyricism. Listen to the lines that close the first act. It is Valya's wedding night.

CHORUS (very softly): The rain is pouring down as if it were about to flood the earth! Little streams are flowing past the houses, washing away the litter and refuse of yesterday. The rain is cleansing the earth. . . .

(Curtain)

These lines occur early in the next act, after the birth of the twins:

CHORUS (sternly): Hush! Do not disturb these citizens. They are still very, very small. . . . It's all right for you who have already grown up and can do without much sleep. But these young citizens must sleep their fill. Do not disturb them. They are only one month old. . . . No, two months . . . No, three. Hush. They must sleep and build up their strength. They are still very small, these little Seryogins.

(The lullaby ceases)

The Chorus, as we see, guides us through the passage of time. At another spot, it does so in this manner:

CHORUS: Now the night is fading, and morning is dawning! Autumn is followed by winter, and then comes the spring. April! A cold windy April, yet spring nevertheless. The last snowflakes rapidly melt in the sun!

Their closing address to the audience is couched in the same kind of familiar, nostalgic simplicity that Wilder used to such great effect:

CHORUS: And while everyone is waiting for Valya's answer, up- stairs in Larissa's room the two young Seryogins, Fyodor and Lena, are fast asleep.

(The familiar lullaby is heard, with voices humming the melody)

They sleep, and their dreams are such as you and I will never see again. Fyodor is dreaming of a little yellow flower he saw that day for the first time in his life. It was sticking up out of the ground beside his little boot. And Lena is dreaming of the blue ball which the boy Anton gave her this morning, the boy who is going to be a doctor.

Like *Our Town, An Irkutsk Story* tells of birth, love, marriage, and death. It has, as an added ingredient, the joy of work and of the comradeship that goes with work. It is here that such Communist propaganda as the play possesses is expressed. But the propaganda does not seem to me to be intrusive, especially in view of the fact that the play is an attempt at a lyrical expression of human life as it is lived in Russia today.

A few weeks later, I went to see this same play produced by Okhlopkov at the Mayakovski Theatre. The contrast between Okhlopkov's style and that of young Yevgeny Simonov, who had directed the Vakhtangov's presentation, was intense. There was certainly no sign of regimentation in Soviet staging as one looked first at one performance, then at the other. The Vakhtangov's production had taken place entirely behind the proscenium; Okhlopkov's production projected itself into the heart of the audience. In contrast to the runway at the Vakhtangov, the runway at the Mayakovski stretched straight through the center of the entire house over a narrow section of orchestra seats, covering the entire distance from the front of the stage to the back of the auditorium. Entrances were effected not only down this runway, but also from the orchestra pit and from proscenium boxes, as well as from the wings. The curtain had been abolished. Here, the Chorus was enlarged from the Vakhtangov's four to one of at least twenty men and women who sat on the stage throughout the play. At first, these members of the Chorus seemed to be part of the audience, for they wandered out of the wings in twos and threes in street clothes and took their seats before the performance started. As the play began, one found them assuming their choral role, until at the finale they became a musical choir that, with the assistance of two thundering pianos and heavy drum rolls, did much to contribute to the epic quality of the production. As in the Vakhtangov production, a revolving stage was used, but in the Mayakovski the revolutions transported actors beyond the line of the proscenium. There was an especially effective quality about the use of the revolving stage in this particular play in both the Vakhtangov and the Mayakovski productions. The rhythm of movement, as the stage brought objects and people forward into focus and then swung them away again into the distance, enhanced the strongly retrospective passing-in-review tone of the drama.

Twenty-five years ago, love stories like *An Irkutsk Story* were unheard of in Soviet repertoires, and I left Moscow at that time complaining that there was a desperate need for romanticism to moderate the "prolonged dose of dialectic materialism." "Surely," I cried then, "the people can afford to take a little time for romancing."

Now I have got what I asked for. The only trouble is that much of the time I have it on a soap-opera level. Plays like *An Irkutsk Story*, films like *Ballad of a Soldier,* both superior to the Russian average, are nonetheless "tear jerkers." The dramatization of Erich Remarque's *Three Comrades* is one of the most popular items in the repertoire of the Ermolova Theatre. But as it comes across on the stage, it has all the earmarks of a latter-day *Camille;* the audience is dissolved in tears at the death of the consumptive Patricia in the arms of her Robert. Sentiment, it seems to me, is separated from sentimentality largely by degree, the latter being but a vulgarization of the former. If the Russians can say with some justification that our modern theatre is decadent; theirs, I feel free to assert, is vulgar. The delicacy, the taste of a Chekhov, who knew how to distinguish between sentiment and sentimentality, are widely lacking in Moscow's theatres today.

This is the price to be paid when one dedicates one's talents to the satisfaction of the masses. Our own daytime television drama and Moscow's contemporary stage drama are, in standard of taste, about equal. The outstanding exception is Obraztsov's Puppet Theatre, but then it has room for only three hundred and fifty spectators, and can thus afford to be caviar to the general.

In a comparison between Soviet drama and America's television output, it is, however, only the sentimentality and tastelessness of each that can be equated. By contrast, Soviet drama has a purposeful intensity and a sense of dedication to more than sheer entertainment that are unknown to the television world of the United States. For Russian sentimental drama always contains an overlay of social orientation. Hero and heroine are united not only in their lives but in their work and in their fidelity to a cause above and beyond their preoccupation with each other. This social orientation derives, of course, not only from the Marxist interpretation of art's *raison d'être,* but from the stage's involvement for so many years with socialist realism. Despite the "thaw" that has allowed a wider latitude in interpreting and applying this style, socialist realism remains, even in such work as *An Irkutsk Story,* the dominant form.

The Russian utilization of realism is today widely at variance with our own. In America, realism seems, more often than not, to lead into an intense preoccupation with degeneracy and with sex. In the name of realism we are offered a spate of dramas that expose us to all manner of practices and perversions, from dope addiction to homosexuality, from incest to cannibalism. We sometimes call it sophistication, but I am tempted to assert that our theatre's current preoccupation with sexuality is rather a reflection of a disjointed society and a jaded appetite. Do we not to some extent deserve the Communists' contemptuous tag of "decadent"?

By contrast, Russian realism moves in precisely the opposite direction. One might be tempted, in fact, to apply the word puritanical to the Russian attitude toward sex, except that this word implies a moral censure which I do not believe enters into it. Prudery does not seem quite apt either, for it suggests a kind of Victorian hypocrisy which is also absent. The Russian attitude is rather one based on a natural reticence regarding the subject, and on a reluctance to flaunt sex openly and discuss it boldly. It is an attitude which is perhaps common to simple folk everywhere. I am sure that a performance of *Sweet Bird of Youth* would shock the sensibilities of my up-country farmer neighbors in Vermont in the same way that it would offend a Moscow audience.

Far from being a degenerate or a psychopath, the hero of every Soviet drama (except in works of satire) is a positive character whose story, in nine cases out of ten, ends happily. He is a man who is, as Edward Weeks, the editor of the *Atlantic Monthly,* described him when speaking about Soviet fiction, "a Galahad in his relations with everyone, who never cheats; who is, indeed, a very boring person." This positive hero may not always start off positively; indeed there may be a second character—an older and wiser man or a good woman—who will effect a change in the hero so that he becomes admirable. In such a case, the Galahadism is delivered in a double dose. This is the usual formula in all the plays about Lenin. In Pogodin's *Kremlin Chimes,* for instance, the protagonist is one Zabelin, a Russian engineer and scientist of the old regime. Distrustful of the Revolution, he is far from a positive hero; but under the magic of Lenin's personality, he is transformed, and by the final curtain he has become a staunch advocate of communism. In many plays in the Central Children's Theatre, the hero starts off as a recalcitrant youth who, like Kolka in Khmelik's *My Friend*

Kolka, turns into a model boy under the influence of a positive character. If a pre-Revolutionary play like *The Cherry
Orchard,* for instance, contains no positive hero, then socialist
realism requires a reinterpretation, so that Lopakhin, the
estate steward who buys up the orchard and dispossesses the
original owners and who is the nearest thing to a positive
character in that drama, may become the heroic man of
tomorrow.

Furthermore, this positive hero cannot fail. Even if he
dies for the cause of Revolution, as happens, for instance, in
Korneichuk's *Wreck of the Squadron* about the Civil War or
in Simonov's *The Russian People* about World War II, his
cause wins through; and everyone leaves the theatre feeling
better for his example, and confident that things are on the
up-and-up.

The obvious result of this practice is unfortunately to rob
drama of its suspense. If one knows in advance that everything will turn out for the best in what will soon be the best
of all possible worlds, one cannot become deeply absorbed in
the conflicts and clashes in which the hero is embroiled. If the
protagonist is heroic to begin with, then there is no change
possible in his character, and such a situation is essentially
undramatic; if he is unheroic, then the only place for him to
go is up, and that becomes boring when his destination is
known in advance. I think it is this insistence on affirmation
that becomes so wearying, both to the foreign observer and
to the Russians themselves. For, even more than the rest of
us, the Russians love a good cry: The more prolonged the
pain and the anguish, the better they like it. The Communists would, of course, have the world believe that they
have changed the character of the Russian people, that tears
give way to smiles, that the earlier Russian tendency to
despair has turned to confidence. To a certain extent this may
be true, though I believe that optimism, too, has always been

an ingredient of the Russian character, one of the several traits the Slavs share with Americans. In any event, just as one wearies of the omnipresence of the happy worker murals and the upward-gazing, muscle-bound banner carriers in sculpture, so one gets terribly weary in the theatre of conventional Browning pap suitable only for Pippa.

The case of *Dr. Zhivago* is not an unrelated one. When the editorial board of the magazine, *Novy Mir,* published its letter refusing Pasternak's manuscript in 1958, it revealed that its chief objection to that extraordinary work was its lack of affirmation: "The spirit of your novel is that of non-acceptance of the Socialist Revolution . . . that, far from having any positive significance in the history of our people and mankind, the October Socialist Revolution brought nothing but evil and hardships." Anyone who has read *Dr. Zhivago* knows the editors of *Novy Mir* speak correctly. Their remarkable letter states their case in such terms as make clear the underlying need of the Russians to feel that in their world, even as in St. Paul's so different world of "them that love the Lord," all things must work together for good.

It is perhaps impossible to expect tragedy to be written in contemporary Russia. Tragedy is not really being written anywhere, for that matter, but Moscow is the least likely place to find its resurgence. For tragedy demands in every time and place, it seems to me, a sure belief in absolute good and evil, that is to say in moral order. Today, relativism has taken over: There is no belief in absolute good and absolute evil, as there is little certain faith in a higher power. For the last hundred years or more, all of us, including the Russians, have seen these things slip away as the result of philosophical, psychological, scientific, social, and political influences to which we have been, to varying degrees, subjected in common.

Hegel's contention that everything is in a state of movement either toward growth or toward decay, that there is
nothing which is not becoming—that is, which is not in an
intermediate position between being and non-being—long ago
provided us with the first step away from a belief in absolutes. Darwin's doctrine of the evolutionary development of
the species, with its emphasis on the survival of the fittest,
took us a step farther. When the monkey replaced Adam and
Eve as our progenitor, when man was thus farther removed
from his exalted position as the center of creation, when he
came to believe that he who wins, wins not through heroism
or greatness of spirit but because he can best adapt to his
environment, man's sense of his own worth and dignity and
of his moral responsibility was, at least for the time being,
reduced.

On top of this came modern psychology. When we accepted
its teachings that our instincts turn back to the past, that
psychological stimuli and responses dictate our actions, that
our subconscious directs our conscious will, then the significance of our deeds tended to become minimized, and our
already reduced sense of moral responsibility and of sin was
still further undermined. "If man—any man—is as he is
because of ten thousand laws of heredity and environment,
then he is not to blame if he fails in life," wrote Frank O'Hara
in *Today in American Drama*. "For after all he is only a
spinning top on a spinning earth in a spinning universe for
which he is certainly not responsible. Even on the stage, it is
not convincing to ask an individual to sacrifice himself for
standards which are based upon blind mechanics or cosmic
futility."

Finally, though not in chronological sequence, came Marx
and Engels. In establishing their theory of economic deter-
minism, they trumpeted anew the general denial of per-

manent values. "Dialectical philosophy," cried Engels, "dis-
solves all conceptions of final, absolute truth and of a final
absolute state of humanity corresponding to it. For it, nothing is final, absolute, sacred. It reveals the transitory character of everything and in everything."

Preoccupation with the relation of the individual to his
social environment is not, of course, exclusive to the Communists. Ibsen and all the nineteenth-century social dramatists down to Odets, Rice, Kingsley, and Miller in this century
in our own country explored society's effect on man and vice
versa. But environment is not a substitute for God, and man's
relation to society is not the same thing as his relation to
some higher spiritual power. "Tragedy's one essential," as
Edith Hamilton expresses it, "is a soul that can feel greatly."

I have already stated my conviction that these influences—
deriving from the teachings of Hegel, Darwin, Freud, Marx,
and Engels—have affected the entire world. I do not believe
that the disappearance of high tragedy from the stage during
these same one hundred and fifty years is coincidental. I do
believe, however, that it is possible for the West to reassert
its recognition of good and evil as moral absolutes and, consequently, to reacquire a climate propitious to the reëmerg-
ence of tragedy. In the West, two basic and precious concepts continue to exist: Christianity and the inviolability of
the individual. By a strengthening of the former and a reaffirmation of the latter, it will eventually be possible for us
to live with the teachings of Hegel and Darwin and Freud
and Marx, and to repossess our own souls in greatness. But
I do not believe this can happen in the Communist world,
where good and evil have only social significance. The Communist East denies both Christianity and the preëminent
worth of the individual above and beyond society. Indeed,
George Steiner tells us in *The Death of Tragedy* that "Luna-

charsky, the first Soviet commissar of education, proclaimed
that one of the defining qualities of a communist society
would be the absence of tragic drama."

Contemporary Soviet dramatists neither attain nor aspire
to the heights of tragedy nor the depths of degradation. Instead, the majority lodge themselves firmly in the middle
ground of the workaday world. There is, in consequence,
such a host of domestic dramas and domestic comedies now
on the boards in Moscow as would tax the endurance of the
most hardened visitor. In a word, they add up to a reflection
of the mores of a society which is constantly assuming a more
bourgeois mien and a more ostensibly Victorian morality.

These dramas may be infinitely boring to us, but then, I
suppose, such slightly risqué domestic comedies as our own
The Seven-Year Itch, The Pleasure of His Company, and
The Marriage-Go-Round, which have delighted thousands of
Americans, would be infinitely boring to the Russians. Even
as we decry the melodramatic and the soap-opera tendencies
in Moscow dramaturgy, let us pause to recall the months
upon months that *The World of Suzie Wong* only recently
reigned as a box-office triumph on Broadway and in London—
then cast the first stone, if we dare.

Domestic drama has not, however, altogether superseded
plays about the life of work. In the thirties, these latter
dramas held almost undisputed sway, so that the Moscow
stage was filled with problems of collective farms, of hydroelectric operations, of factory management, and of railroads.
A country that was attempting to turn itself overnight into
an industrial nation made full use of the theatre to express
the national preoccupation and to instill enthusiasm for its
goals. Nowadays, there are still a few of the older type of
work dramas to be seen, but factories and farms really serve

today principally as backgrounds for human dramas, in which, as one Communist critic tries to explain, "the poetry of labor is naturally linked with true life."

Such a contemporary play is *Son of the Century* by Ivan Kuprianov. This young author with workman's hands and a seamy but open, friendly face began his career as a laborer in a Siberian hydroelectric plant, so it is not surprising that his play is concerned with problems of life on such a project. The drama he poses is at the heart of Soviet life today: the honest conflict between the old way and the new; between the sincere and intelligent director of the project, who has been trained to believe that the fulfillment of his "quota" must be his prime objective and responsibility, versus the new local Party representative, who places the personal welfare of the workers above the impersonal demands of the quota.

What this play does is to dramatize the conflict between the Stalinists and their successors. Naturally, the latter win, for this is today's "line." Kuprianov has, however, the unexpected wisdom to paint a full and sympathetic portrait of a man whose life has been molded by the belief, instilled in him throughout the thirties and the forties and a part of the fifties, that doing one's assigned job, to the maximum of one's ability and at all costs,—including, if need be, the sacrifice of all concern for the personal, spiritual, and physical well-being of the individual workers in one's charge—is a goal that must override all others. Here, uniquely, is a play with a conflict in which the two points of view are very nearly evenly balanced.

Son of the Century opened in Kazan, some three thousand miles east of Moscow. In 1960, it was being performed in sixty-four theatres throughout the Soviet Union. The performance I saw in Moscow was at the Gogol Theatre, in one of the more remote working quarters of the city. Since the

drama's problem has more immediacy in places where the
circumstances described in it are occurring, it is more successful in the provinces than in Moscow or Leningrad.

Equally popular in both province and metropolis are the
plays of Victor Rozov, which are also concerned, in a different
and more universal context, with the conflict between the
old and the new. For Rozov treats of the rising younger generation, whose problems are the same whether they live in
Kazan or in Moscow. This slender, short, slightly balding, energetic young playwright is among the wealthiest of
Soviet citizens, a circumstance he owes to the very fact that
his plays are performed so widely and that he draws royalties
from them all (at least four of his works were produced
simultaneously on Moscow stages during the 1960–1961
season).

The secret of Rozov's popularity lies, in my opinion, in
the fact that he understands the younger postwar generation,
even in some cases the post-Stalin generation, better than do
most contemporary dramatists. Too young to fight, the
members of this generation were evacuated and protected
during World War II; they grew up in the forties, reached
their majority in the fifties. Naturally, they are therefore
different from their predecessors, who were the young men
and women between the wars. One of their chief problems,
in consequence, appears to be that of being understood by
their parents, their teachers, and their employers.

What is involved in Rozov's plays, in point of fact, is the
whole question of the evolving Soviet society. The shock
which Khrushchev's destruction of the Stalin image gave to
the Soviet people can only be partially realized by the West. It
cut the ground out from under the faith of the entire older
generation, and it instilled in the new one a sense that their
elders were not, after all, infallible. Of course, younger generations the world over are infected by this delicious malady,

but seldom have they had such good cause as these young Russians. Rozov has addressed himself to this public, and in reply they turn out in droves to listen to him. On two sides of Theatre Square, as old Sverdlov Square has been renamed, stand the Maly and the Children's theatres. Both are presenting Rozov's *Uneven Combat*. The latter theatre is attended largely by teen-agers, attracted by the fact that its protagonist is a boy of about sixteen; while the Maly's production is attended by all ages, who are engrossed in the youngster's problem of finding himself. Another popular Rozov play is one entitled *Good Luck,* which again treats of the problems of the younger generation—of a young Communist's choice of his life work, of his first love, and of his quest for Communist happiness.

So, too, the problems of adjustment between the generations are a part of Alexander Volodin's *At Home and Visiting.* Yet it is elsewhere that the most significant aspect of this apparently unimportant drama lies. The story is of a widow with two teen-age children, who falls deeply in love with a distinguished academician. He stands ready to marry her, but she refuses to commit herself. The youngsters, disturbed by the unresolved situation, leave home, and, taking refuge with family friends, discover that they have fallen from the frying pan into the fire. Their benefactors, it turns out, are a narrow, bigoted, self-righteous couple whose rigid code, based on snobbism and external appearances, allows no place for tolerance. Finally, everything ends happily when, reconciling themselves to their mother, the children return home.

The significance of *At Home and Visiting* lies in the fact that it contains an only slightly concealed plea for personal freedom, even when such freedom runs counter to the accepted code. A play that calls for the greater freedom of the individual in the U.S.S.R. should not be underestimated. Yet, not only is the play allowed to run, but it is performed more

frequently than any other play in the Ermolova Theatre's
repertoire, and always to sold-out houses. As drama, *At Home
and Visiting* is negligible; as a social document, it is far from
negligible.

The conflict between the generations was exposed in play
after play during the 1960–1961 Moscow season, and one of
the most effective treatments of this theme was to be seen in
the Central Children's Theatre's production of *My Friend
Kolka*. I have always been attracted to the Central Children's
Theatre, as much because of the audience as because of what
happens onstage. I love to watch the demure little girls in
their white pinafores with white organdy bows on their pig-
tails, and the exuberant boys in their blue-gray Pioneer uni-
forms with scarlet neckerchiefs, who keep standing up whenever the action gets exciting.

But I do not mean to belittle what happens across the footlights, for the standard of production in the Central Children's Theatre is, and always has been, extremely high. In
My Friend Kolka, the curtain rises on a panorama of a play-
ground where, in almost choreographed action, boys and
girls are to be seen jumping and sliding, throwing balls, playing tag, and chinning themselves on bars, as the revolving
stage swings around to the strains of Prokofiev's *Peter and the
Wolf*. Behind the stage there is a stylized background of the
city skyline, painted lettuce green and vermilion and white.

The play is another contemporary piece about a restless
young teen-ager who is repelled by unimaginative con-
formity. It might have been of his life that David Burg (the
pseudonym of a young Russian scholar who left the U.S.S.R.
to settle in the West) wrote in May, 1961, when he said, "As
for the [high school] students, there was a distinct atmosphere
of boredom at the Komsomol meetings. Endless propagandistic talk of national aims, the duties of youth, the same
phrases repeated over and over again, and most felt it was a

tremendous waste of time. Nothing happened that anyone really cared about much, in a personal way." Kolka, however, finally finds his way toward his place in Soviet life through the sympathetic guidance of a young man who understands the reasons for his rebellion, sympathizes with him, and provides him with an alternative to the "endless propagandistic talk." What might itself sound like sermonizing comes forth in this production, directed by Anatoly Efros, as real-life comedy-melodrama. Extraordinarily good young actors, some still apprentices in this theatre and still below the age of twenty, play the youngsters with no sense of histrionics, but just as though the action were the real thing. The audience takes it in the same spirit.

When Edward Weeks said, in describing the role of criticism in Soviet literature, that it is "directed at inefficiency in people, but no higher than the chairman of a coöperative farm," he was, I believe, only partially right. For I suspect that he had not heard of Yevgeny Schwarz, that master satirist who died in 1958, nor had he heard of *The Naked King* or *The Dragon*, the former one of the several Hans Christian Andersen fairy tales that Schwarz has adapted for the stage, the latter a hodge-podge of myths whose principal character is Sir Lancelot. For Schwarz's purposes, Lancelot is less an Arthurian knight than a member of the age-old, dragon-slaying company of St. George and Perseus.

I did not hear of Schwarz until shortly before I left Moscow. His name is not once mentioned in Komissarzhevski's *Moscow Theatres*. *The Naked King* was given a single closed performance by the Sovremennik Theatre; otherwise Schwarz was unproduced in Moscow during my stay in 1960. No performance of *The Dragon*, in fact, has ever been permitted in the Soviet Union, although a script of the play was published in a collection of Schwarz's works that came out (and immediately sold out) in 1960. Once I became aware of him and mentioned his name, however, a number of the most discriminating and intelligent of my theatrical friends readily admitted that he might well be Russia's most brilliant dramatist.

Why the secrecy? Why had Schwarz never been mentioned earlier? The answer apparently lies in the fact that he has managed to come closer to looking critically at the Soviet regime than has anyone else in modern Russia. Take his version of *The Emperor's New Clothes,* which he has entitled *The Naked King.* In it, he tells essentially the the same old story. A king orders a couple of young men who are disguised as tailors to make him the most beautiful suit anyone has ever seen. Since the youths have no idea how to cut and sew, they oblige with invisible raiment, and the entire court is obsequiously enthusiastic when the vain king dons nothing and parades himself before them naked. Only among his lesser subjects does one little child cry, "But the king has nothing on," and, after a shocked gasp, everyone begins to laugh, for indeed the king *has* nothing on. If this is not exactly political satire, it comes as close to it as anything I have ever seen—or am likely to see—in a country where everyone is constantly congratulating the government on its omniscience; where no one questions the supreme authority; where, when the ruler rides naked, no little child's piping voice is heard to bring the people to their senses.

As is obvious, Schwarz's treatment of this and other Andersen stories, including *The Shadow* and *The Snow Queen,* is as straight fairy tales, enlivened with even more wry wit than that with which their Danish originator endowed them. There is no need to preach nor to draw a parallel nor to point a moral. There is no need to dress the characters in modern clothes. As long as the whole thing is kept as fantasy, author and public alike can always claim it is innocuous and means nothing. But I doubt very much that the public I saw at *The Naked King* thought it meant nothing. A reading of the text of *The Dragon* also makes it unavoidably clear that in this play Schwarz had the Stalinist Terror in mind, when he wrote of a fear-ridden city which cowered under the bloody talons of a dragon; that for the character of the Burgomaster, who imposed new authority on the populace after Sir Lancelot had slain the dragon and freed the populace, Khrushchev might have been the model had the play not have been written in 1943 before his accession to power.

At the Theatre of Satire I saw Vladimir Mayakovski's *The Bedbug*, which made such a stir in 1955 when it was revived after being absent from the stage for twenty-five years. To be sure, Stalin had, in 1935, hailed the poet who had committed suicide five years earlier at the age of thirty-seven, as "the best and most talented of our epoch," but the Communists were always uncomfortable in the presence of Mayakovski's astringent wit, especially when it was turned not against capitalism but, as Patricia Blake has said, against ". . . the Soviet bourgeoisie: the profiteers, the Party fat cats, the proletarian philistines." It is illustrative of the changing times that at the end of the fifties Mayakovski's work was once again being received as a smashing success. And at the Theatre of Satire today, not only Mayakovski's *The Bedbug*, but also his *The Bathhouse* and *Mystery Bouffe* are being performed.

The Bedbug is the story of one Prisypkin, a cheerful dolt, brilliantly and broadly played by a great clown, V. Lepko. Although a Party card carrier, Prisypkin is no epitome of the "new man," but a "bedbug-infested, guitar-strumming, vodka-soaked vulgarian" with illusions of bourgeois grandeur. "I'm a man of higher needs," he cries. "What I'm interested in is a wardrobe with a mirror." He is also interested in acquiring a rich wife, and he finds her in the person of Elzevir Davidovna Renaissance. "Elzevir—that's the name of a type face," remarks one of Prisypkin's cronies, to whom his buddy replies, "I don't know about her type face, but she's certainly got a figure." So Prisypkin wins his typographical Elzevir, but not for long. Their wedding breakfast, in one of the most hilarious low-comedy scenes ever staged, is brought to an inflammatory end when one of the ushers, who has accidentally stuck a fish down the bosom of the bride, pushes her into the stove while trying to extricate it. The whole scene goes up in flames along with the wedding veil.

The second half of the story takes place fifty years later, in a Mayakovski version of George Orwell's *1984*. Instead of being burned up, Prisypkin, it turns out, had been frozen solid in the avalanche of water with which the fire department had extinguished the blaze. (It was a cold night.) Discovered in this state, our hero is defrosted into a Communist millennium of 1979, where he is looked upon as a zoological freak by a sterile, automated society. Thus he is finally forced to exchange his hibernation in an ice cake for life in a cage, from behind whose bars he cries out to the audience, "Citizens! Brothers! My own people! Darlings! How did you get here? . . . Why am I alone in the cage? Darlings, friends, come and join me! Why am I suffering?" It is, however, the director of the zoo who has the last word in a wry, tragicomic conclusion. "My apologies, comrades . . ." he announces. "The noise and the bright lights gave [Prisypkin] hallucinations. Please be calm. . . . Disperse quietly, citizens, until tomorrow. Music. Let's have a march!"

And the curtain falls.

In this production it is interesting to note the marriage of Mayakovski's literary style with a resurgence of Meierhold's theatrical style. In point of fact, the play can be presented only with the kind of wild theatricality of which Meierhold

was a master. Thus the production establishes its time and
setting—the New Economic Policy (N.E.P.) period of the
1920's—at the beginning of the performance by means of a
kaleidoscope of petit-bourgeois figures, each outlandishly
caricatured, who pass before us on a conveyor belt; and the
later scenery, depicting the laboratories and streets of 1979,
is as abstract and anti-illusionistic as Meierhold could have
wished, with a plethora of shadows and whirling lights projected on the backdrop. In keeping with the style of Meierhold, the proscenium seldom figures in the proceedings:
Firemen run down the aisles to put out the conflagration,
which brings the first part of the play to its climax; in the
second act, newsboys shout their headlines throughout the
auditorium, as they run up one aisle and down another:

> Read how the man froze
> Lead stories in verse and prose!

> Feature on ancient guitars and romances
> And other means of drugging the masses!

> *Science Gazette! Science Gazette!*
> Theoretical discussion of ancient problem—
> Can an elephant die from a cigarette?

And in the midst of it all, Prisypkin darts through the house
in search of his runaway bedbug, which had survived with
him in the ice cake, finally pinning it down on a balcony rail
with a shout of triumph. It's a wild night at the Theatre of
Satire!

At the Variety Theatre, I witnessed satire in a different
garb, in a show called, inexplicably, *From Two to Fifty*,
which had been written by three men, M. Ginden, K. Ryzhov,
and G. Ryabkin, for an extremely talented actor named
Arkady Raikin. Like any good topical revue, *From Two to
Fifty* had its fun at the expense of all manner of pertinent

subjects—from the service of waitresses in Soviet restaurants to progressive education, alcoholism, housing problems, and love. Social satire it was, though political satire it was not.

The show was really an intimate revue with a small orchestra, presenting only a cast of twelve in addition to Raikin himself, who appeared not only as the master of ceremonies, with a running commentary of jokes, anecdotes, and some elaborate monologues, but also as a character in all but four of the sketches or musical numbers. Raikin's base of operations is Leningrad, but when this small, Puckish fellow with the big mouth and the shyly ironic smile—a sort of flesh-and-blood Charlie McCarthy—comes to town for a two- or three-month engagement, every Muscovite who can wangle a seat is on hand to laugh and cheer. It was the first time I had seen a satirical revue in Moscow, and it stands up very well in comparison with our own.

Since Soviet dramaturgy is supposed both to reflect the people's lives and to guide their thinking, it should be valuable to scan the present-day theatre for clues to the Russian attitude toward the future and especially toward peace. Basing my judgment on the cross section of performances I attended in the U.S.S.R. in 1960, it would seem that the Soviet theatre is not preoccupied with the prospect of war, that it gives less thought to the morrow than it did a quarter of a century ago, and that, when it does express itself on the subject, it proclaims a belief in "peaceful coexistence."

As early as 1935, there were plays in Moscow that were patently designed to foment distrust of Nazi Germany. True, too, in the early years of the cold war, there were, I am told, a number of anti-American plays on the boards. But today the only really anti-American ones are those by Lillian Hellman and Arthur Miller, and that is so only because the Russians have so misunderstood the material that it comes out upside down. Actually, the fact is that whatever indictment is made of America in *A View from the Bridge, A Memory of Two Mondays, Death of a Salesman,* and *The Autumn Garden* (and I believe it is slight in these particular plays) comes as a result of a series of cliché conceptions of the Capitalist world that puts one in mind of the comic strips, as, for example, in the case of Linda Loman in *Death of a Salesman,* who in the Russian version is dressed in satin and pearls as she washes the breakfast dishes.

I saw only one example of the Russian attitude toward the future, in *The Sword of Damocles* by the Turkish dramatist, Nazim Hikmet. This drama, although no satire, is part of the repertoire of the Theatre of Satire in Moscow. But it is also widely performed throughout the Soviet Union. If one did not know it was already on the boards in May, 1960, one would assume it had been written to order after the U-2 incident.

In this play a Russian couple receive a letter from a young American friend. As they read the lengthy epistle, which is both a confession and a warning, the contents of the letter are enacted, becoming the main body of the play. The couple's young friend has written to tell them that, through an infatuation with a girl, he has found himself framed by government agents, who on this stage resemble the Hollywood trench-coated-and-slouched-hat image of gangsters, and that he has been forced by them into becoming a flier. The letter warns the Russian couple that he is heading toward them in a sneak attack, carrying the surprise hydrogen bomb that will unleash the next war.

The theatre fills with the noise of the approaching plane. I have never heard stereophonic sound used to such terrifying effect. The theatre rocks with the reverberation of the airplane's engines. The couple cling to each other; the audience trembles. Then the engines diminish, and the plane passes

over. In a few moments the young American pilot bursts in:
At the last moment he could not obey his orders to release the
bomb. Humanity is too precious. The curtain falls, and the
audience cheers.

I do not know what kind of propaganda this is supposed
to be. What it adds up to is engrossing melodrama, and a conclusion which apparently succeeds in reassuring the Russian
audience that no matter how war-mongering the American
government is, when the chips are down the American people
will not go along with it. It comforts a public that I am
convinced does not believe in the depths of its heart that
America is aggressively-minded. I think the drama feeds a
desire for peace in the Russian people, which I believe to be
genuine.

Of all the artists of the Soviet theatre, its dramatists make
the least distinguished contribution. This was true in the
thirties and it is still true. I am not sure, however, whether it
is fair to claim that the dramatists are the least able of Soviet
artists. Perhaps it is circumstance that confines them, not lack
of ability. Obviously the playwright, who provides the theatre
with its content, whose task it is to convert ideas and attitudes
and feelings and a concept of life into dramatic form, who
makes his statement and commits himself through the written
word, feels the pressure of thought control in a way that
other artists of the theatre need not experience.

If freedom of speech truly existed in the Soviet Union,
playwriting might assume its proper place among the contributing arts that combine to make theatre. But this is only
a matter of conjecture. Certainly, the Soviet theatre reached
its world preëminence in the 1920's and early 1930's in spite
of its playwrights. But that accomplishment is very nearly
unique in the long history of the stage, and it took place in
large measure because, on one hand, the rest of the world

also had very few playwrights of great stature during those years (Shaw, who was approaching his twilight, O'Casey, and O'Neill being the only ones in all the West) and, on the other hand, because other countries had few theatrical leaders of the caliber of Stanislavski, Nemirovich-Danchenko, Meierhold, Vakhtangov, and Tairov.

Exactly what is the status of the writer's "freedom of speech" in Russia today? In Moscow in the thirties, one was very much aware of the so-called "Glavrepertkom" or Chief Repertory Committee of the government. To it, all manuscripts proposed for production were submitted for approval before being put into work. At a run-through prior to the première, the Repertkom inspected the final result in order to make sure that no subversive interpretation had either consciously or unconsciously infiltrated an acceptable play. When I inquired about the Repertkom in 1960, I was told it had been abolished. At that time each theatre was free to produce whatever plays it pleased. "The Repertkom served a useful purpose in its day," explained Alexander N. Kuznetsov, the Deputy Minister of Culture, when the subject was brought up, "for in those years there were many artists who did not understand the Revolution or the meaning of socialism. Now everyone does, so there is no need for the government to advise them. Today, there is no official censorship over our theatre."

I take this statement at its face value, which does not mean, I hope, that I am taken in by it. In the first place, it is my impression that today the large majority of dramatists and theatre leaders do "understand the Revolution and the meaning of socialism," and that, furthermore, they are devoted to its future and committed to its ends. They are neither tempted to write subversively nor to produce subversive material any more than American dramatists and managers are tempted to write and produce plays which the House

Un-American Activities Committee would call subversive. A look over last season's list of plays presented on and off Broadway in New York will fail to uncover any expression of anti-American sentiment. Certainly, there may have been plays implicitly or explicitly critical of American morals and mores, as in Edward Albee's *The American Dream,* for example, but such plays were not challenging the political status quo. The vast majority of our fellow citizens accept the American political way of life; the vast majority of the Russians accept theirs. There is no need for the government to advise them any more than there is need of censorship of our theatre to insure the safety of the Republic.

This is not to say, however, that there is no counterrevolutionary sentiment in the Soviet Union, nor that there are no anti-Communists. I am sure that there are, just as there are doubtless pro-Communists in the United States. And it is quite possible that, if there were true freedom of speech, others beside Boris Pasternak and Yevgeny Schwarz might rise up and give utterance to their disenchantment. For, of course, even though the Repertkom has been abolished, everyone knows that dissenters against the Communist Party line get short shrift. That is why it is now possible to say that theatres are free to produce whatever they choose. If, perchance, they were to choose plays which were not pleasing to the state (like Schwarz's *The Dragon,* let us say), the examples of Meierhold and Pasternak stand to remind them of what might happen. It is thus, of course, impossible to know how many artists are muzzled by this built-in censorship.

This is essentially the generation of the sons and daughters of Doctor Zhivago, who have accepted the Revolution and become a part of it; and this present-day acceptance is, in fact, related to one of the principal changes I have already noted in the content of Soviet drama over the past twenty-five years. Propaganda has ceased to play its overtly persuasive role. No longer is one exposed to those crude plays that quickened the blood with their portrayal of the heroic exploits of the glorious Reds against the infamous Whites in the Civil War. Seldom is one exhorted to make common cause against a common enemy (the enemy ranging from Capitalist infiltration to mismanagement of hydroelectric plants). I did not even hear in the autumn of 1960 a direct word of anti-American propaganda on any Moscow stage, although the daily press was full of it and Mr. Khrushchev was loudly voicing it at the United Nations.

I think the reduction of propaganda in the theatre relates not only to the fact that the public is already persuaded, but also to the fact that because it is persuaded, it is bored by the broadside attack. People, I am convinced, go to *An Irkutsk Story* not to applaud the Socialist message that its conclusion preaches, but to weep over the pathetic love story that ends so sadly. This is not to say that contemporary Soviet drama is no longer concerned with promoting the "building of socialism." It is and always will be, as long as Marxism rules. But the technique of promotion has changed. Moscow has discovered the "soft sell," at least for the home consumer.

If, then, I am persuaded that writers, like the public at large, are committed to communism, how can I attribute the inferiority of contemporary dramatic output to lack of freedom? My answer is that dialectical materialism seems to me to impose a narrowness upon one's vision of man and of life that thwarts the creative spirit. The will to conform is alien to the will to conceive. In yielding his freedom to an omniscient state, even voluntarily or unconsciously, an artist forfeits one of the surest wellsprings of his creativity. I am convinced that this is the reason why in all the arts communism has produced so few great figures.

Perhaps the interpretative artist suffers less under this system; and this may be why Richter and Oistrakh and

Ulanova amaze the world with their performances, and why actors and directors can be praised in a theatre that has no worth-while new drama. These, strictly speaking, are all interpreters of the creations of others. They can express their artistic selves through Beethoven and Chaikovski, through Musorgski and Mozart, through Chekhov and Shakespeare and Molière, even through Rozov and Arbuzov and Schwarz. The statement has been made for them.

I must say that the modern Russian playwright has learned nothing about how to write a play in twenty-five years. I have the same criticism of his technique to make now that I had then: The Soviet playwright has no idea of unity and concentration of material. The Soviet dramatists do not seem to have discovered the fact that the dramatic form and the narrative form are two very different things. By Western standards, the diffuseness of their dramas is incredible. It is reflected not merely in the length of their plays, which is nearly twice that of ours; it is in the way in which they try to include what is to us extraneous material. Possibly this penchant is in keeping with some socialist-realist tenet to the effect that the protagonist should be surrounded by as much of his environment, by as many of his fellow citizens as can be squeezed into three-and-a-half hours. I see no other reason for dragging in the stories of half-a-dozen onlookers to the main event, each with his own little action which, in many cases, the playwright leaves hanging unresolved. Yet this is the popular practice, and, in addition, a Soviet play never seems to know where to begin nor where to end. It proceeds to unfold its story in narrative, not dramatic sequence. Acts appear to come to an end not because a climax has been reached, but because it is time at the end of an hour to give the audience a rest. Then, too, there is little sense of progression in the action, which lumbers slowly through a vast

number of brief episodes. As I said in 1935, "with this diffuseness there comes a good deal of repetition which eventually loses its effectiveness."

There is a picaresque quality to Soviet drama that results
from this approach, but the picaresque has always struck me
as alien to the dramatic. The Russians need to absorb what
Aristotle had to say about "the beginning, the middle, and
the end" and about unity of action. They would do well to
take a second look at the French classical dramatists. In fact,
I think their plight is so desperate that I recommend study
of Scribe and Sardou and of the French "well-made play," a
dose I would prescribe only in extremis. For the Russian
dramatist's problem is principally one of self-discipline and
of the organization of material, and these things they could
learn both from the well-made play and from the classicists.
I have never heard of any Russian seminars in playwriting.
Despite the extraordinary Russian training program for the
stage, the writer has been overlooked. I know of no George
Pierce Baker in the history of the Soviet theatre. Though
nobody would claim that a teacher can create a dramatist,
such a teacher is nevertheless of great help to a talented
writer who needs to learn the rules of this highly exacting art
form.

My other criticism in the thirties was that the Soviet
dramatist also fell short in techniques of characterization.
His chief trouble then was that he tried to paint his people
only in black and white. Today's playwrights have become
more sophisticated. They know that over-simplification leads
to cardboard figures, and they do what they can to give three
dimensions to their characters. That they now succeed better
than they did, I concede; that they could do still better, they
concede. "There is still so much room for improvement,"
writes Victor Rozov in *Sovietskaya Literatura*, "that it would
be absurd to sit back in satisfaction. There are still very few

plays. The fact that *An Irkutsk Story* is running in three
Moscow theatres and my *Uneven Combat* in two is by no
means to be welcomed, flattering as it may seem to be to the
playwright concerned." But when Rozov offers his view of the
goal—"It is up to us to show the world the rich, fine, inner
world of the man of our day, the beauty of his moral character"—I am afraid he is offering us nothing but double-talk,
and I despair of the Russians producing anything that will be
universally exciting and moving.

The Soviet writer, Arkady Anastasyev, in his piece in the
same discussion of "Dramatic Art in Our Day" to which
Rozov was contributing, continues the criticism:

A playwright who wants to disclose a conflict existing in real
life must raise the opposing forces to the height of contradiction,
accentuate the differences between the conflicting forces to an
essential difference, to *oppositeness*.

How is it then that in our dramaturgy the conflicting forces
are not always raised to [this height of contradiction], that the
conflict does not always represent a decisive, mutually dangerous,
meaningful struggle? I think the answer is that all too often art is
wrongfully likened to life, that the truth of real life is identified
with artistic truth.

The theory has been thrown overboard, but in practice we continue to have plays without conflicts. [Yet] now they come in a
guise which I think might best be called *illustrativeness*.

Most generally this illustrativeness takes the form of moralizing
and a mechanical likening of art to life, both [of them] qualities
alien to true art. The writer who does not see that this is a sin
against both life and art is little concerned with presenting a
poetic summary of those things in life that stir his imagination,
with giving expression to their *very essence*. He simply takes one
or several features of real life in their isolated state and transfers
them to his play, poem or canvas in order to denote and illustrate
one or another phenomenon, one or another thesis.

But the drama is not illustration. It is the artistic expression of man's spiritual life as revealed in the concentrated conflict of opposing forces.

That is an excellent statement. In it, a Russian presents my case for me. The drama is, indeed, not illustration. When Soviet playwrights learn that lesson, when they learn from their own Anastasyev that it "is the artistic expression of man's spiritual life as revealed in the concentrated conflict of opposing forces," they will have achieved a measure of maturity that will give them the right to sit among their contemporaries— Russian actors, directors, designers—as their peers.

4

The Old Guard

in 1960

Today, the Maly and the Moscow Art Theatre remain Moscow's two oldest and most distinguished dramatic theatres, and, though neither impresses me now as a central force in the Moscow theatrical world, their seniority and fame accord them first place in any survey of the city's stages. Even in 1935, one of these, the Maly, seemed to stand apart from the mainstream, which was fed principally from five creative springs: the Moscow Art Theatre, the Theatre of Meierhold, the Vakhtangov Theatre, the Kamerny Theatre of Tairov, and the Realistic Theatre in Krasnaya Presnaya. Now the Art Theatre, too, has moved a long way in the direction of becoming—like the Maly—the sort of "academic" theatre that the Comédie Française has until recently been in France, a monument to tradition, a museum that contains some of the nation's most valued treasures, a spot every art lover must visit, but more associated with the past than the present.

I make this judgment of the Moscow Art Theatre with profound reluctance, and I am willing to believe that the future may cause me to alter my opinion. Yet two profoundly important things have happened to the Art Theatre in the last quarter-century, each cataclysmic enough to have destroyed any lesser institution. The first was the death in 1938 of Constantin Sergeyevich Stanislavski, followed a year later by the demise of co-founder Vladimir Ivanovich Nemirovich-Danchenko. The second has been, ironically, the exaltation of the Art Theatre to a position of unquestioned leadership as the arch-exponent of socialist realism by the Party's cultural reactionaries.

Both Stanislavski and Nemirovich actively served their creation up until their last days, and the MXAT* has not yet, some twenty years later, completely recovered from the shock of their passing. Stanislavski foresaw the confusion that might follow his death, and his last years were devoted with increasing vigilance to preparing heirs who might be capable of assuming the mantle of responsibility. It may be said that he had a sense of history. He knew the importance of his contribution to the world's stage even while he lived. He knew, too, that as is the fate of many prophets his words stood open to misinterpretation by succeeding generations. He therefore recognized the necessity of clarifying his thoughts as carefully as possible. Unfortunately, however, he was in the first place a doer rather than a thinker, as one discovers by placing the verbatim transcript of his rehearsals recorded in *Stanislavski Directs* alongside his own theoretical exposition, *An Actor Prepares*. In the second place, his ideas were always changing.

At the beginning, what Stanislavski and Nemirovich-Danchenko had wanted was quite clear, or rather it was quite

* These initials, by which the Moscow Art Theatre is commonly known, stand for the theatre's full name, Moskovski Khudozhestvenny Akademicheski Teatr, which, translated literally, means "Moscow Artistic Academic Theatre." The letter "x" in the abbreviation is the Russian character for the sound of the letters "kh."

clear what they did *not* want: "The program we set out to
implement," Stanislavski has written, "was a revolutionary
one. We were protesting against the old manner of acting,
against theatricality and affected pathos, declamation, and
overacting, against ugly conventionalities of scenery, against
the star system which was harmful for the company, against
the way plays were written, against poor repertoires." What
they *did* want was to follow the injunction of the nineteenth-
century Russian actor Shchepkin, which Stanislavski often
quoted: "Take your models from life and nature." And to
this statement Stanislavski added his own: that it was his
intention "to chase the theatre from the theatre." In 1898,
when the MXAT was founded, until Stanislavski's death, almost forty years later, this protest and this search continued.
For good or bad, the Moscow Art Theatre—together with the
earlier accomplishments of the Saxe-Meiningen troupe (from
which the men in Moscow took many of their ideas) and
André Antoine in Paris, Otto Brahm in Berlin, and, of course,
Ibsen and Strindberg in the north—effected a change in the
European theatre, and subsequently in the American theatre,
which has remained in both to this day.

The problem with which Stanislavski wrestled throughout
his career was what to do with the models the actor finds in
"life and nature," how to bring them to life on the stage
without resorting to that mere mimicry which always seemed
to him both hollow and untrue. His ideas were always changing concerning the proper means to this end. I observed his
system in 1935, but even then—two years before his death—
he told me he was no longer convinced that the methods he
had been using to lead an actor to artistic truth were the best
ones.

Certain practices, to be sure, remained as valid parts of his
system. The actor had to continue to be able to control his
attention, to practice concentration—perhaps by drawing an

invisible circle about himself onstage; he had to be able to develop his imagination and to conjure forth "fantasy," so that he could respond to any given circumstances truthfully, whether he had ever experienced these in his own life or not—from the death of a child, to the chasing of a monkey up a palm tree; he had to retain the naïveté of a child who plays with a doll and pretends it is alive; he had to continue to establish "contact" with his stage partner, to "play to his eyes," really to listen when he spoke. These were basic techniques to practice if the "theatre of inner feeling" were to be realized to the full; but they were only techniques, means to an end. The deeper problems which Stanislavski summed up, I recall, in such phrases as "the superproblem of the role" and finally in "the incarnation" were ones whose challenge was to him never-ending.

I talked of the present-day solutions to these problems in the autumn of 1960 with Mikhail Kedrov, Artistic Director of the Moscow Art Theatre and an old friend of twenty-five years' standing. It was he on whom the mantle of Stanislavski fell. It was he who had worked with the aging master to codify his beliefs and to put them into final book form. Kedrov is a hulking, round-faced man, with thinning gray hair; a quiet, gentle, almost cherubic demeanor; and a shy sense of humor. There are those in Moscow who say that he is not aggressive and dictatorial enough to hold the MXAT firmly together, and this may be one of its troubles.

The heavy furniture of the executive offices of this famous company is fitted with white linen dust covers, winter and summer. The windows of the offices look out across an alley toward the windows of the Nemirovich-Danchenko School, the Art Theatre's training center, of which Kedrov is also the chief and in which he spends many hours teaching, for he has learned well Stanislavski's lesson that the future lies with the young. In this room, whose quiet suggests that noth-

ing ever happens in it, we sat for two hours while he talked
about Stanislavski (for, as a disciple of Constantin Sergeyevich, he tends to underemphasize the importance of Nemirovich-Danchenko) and of the problems of holding the line
at the Art Theatre.

Kedrov likened the Stanislavski system to the old horse-
drawn streetcars that used to carry one out to Sokolniki Park.
The cars and their horses are gone now, and the park, although still there, has also changed. Today the Metro takes
you to that same, but almost unrecognizable, spot. In other
words, Kedrov was explaining that the goal of the Stanislavski
method remains the same, though it looks different, and that
the means to it have altered, though the raison d'être has not.

"I am always amused," he told me, "at the people who say
they understand and practice the Stanislavski system and then
proceed to interpret it in quite different and often contradic-
tory ways. And each one says he is doing what Stanislavski
taught. It all depends, you see, on when they happened to
work with him. He was constantly changing his system—
would still be changing it, I've no doubt, were he still alive.
So the conception which a man who worked with Constantin
Sergeyevich in 1925 took away with him was quite different
from that of a man who worked with him later in 1930 or
still later in 1935. Beware of the fellow who says: '*This* is
what Stanislavski meant.' "

I could not help thinking of the practitioners of "the
Method" in America, who fixed their technique on what
Stanislavski was teaching in the early 1930's (principally
about the means of arriving at psychological truth) and have
maintained its sacrosanctity ever since.

"The basic problem, you see," Kedrov went on, reflectively,
"is to determine what *is* a man. If we are to recreate him on
stage, we must start by asking ourselves this question, and
then the trouble begins. Is it his soul and his body? Do we

begin with this combination? Or does the key to him lie in his emotions, his will, his thoughts? Perhaps we should begin with his skeleton and then add his respiratory, circulatory, and nervous systems, and finally his flesh. Stanislavski kept fluctuating in his search for the key, for the place to begin to create a man, whether he be Othello or a contemporary Soviet citizen."

Stanislavski, according to Kedrov, was early interested in the research being done by Pavlov (so was Meierhold, I recall), and he followed the work of his scientific compatriot carefully, as the latter developed his theories of conditioned reflexes and deterministic behavior. But, in the long run, it is my impression, Stanislavski decided that the will was the basic factor with man: That the will determines behavior, and that the way a man behaves determines what a man is. This point of view, Kedrov confirmed, was set forth by a stage-struck detective, who wrote to Kedrov after reading an article by Stanislavski's disciple describing the esthetic argument: "You're right and the others wrong. We have learned from our police experience that a man's acts—his physical behavior—reveal his true nature. How he looks, what he says can deceive; what he *does* determines it." It would appear, then, that the Stanislavski system finally evolves into a method based on physical action, which is not at all the way we used to interpret it.

But this is not the whole answer. For Kedrov went on to say that Stanislavski continued to remind his followers that, where man is concerned, Pavlov and his reflexes are obviously only a part; motive is always present and must never be lost sight of. "Any actor can burst in through a door, but a good actor will always ask, 'Why?'"

In his recent book, *Moscow Theatres,* Victor Komissarzhevski, a distinguished Soviet director and critic, confirms this reversal of approach. Stanislavski's final conclusion about the key to acting, he says, was that it lay in the deed. The actor "must only perform some very simple physical act, an elementary act as Stanislavski qualified it. That roused his imagination. He required the producer to tell him more and more about his part, to explain his behaviour. The rest was accomplished during the rehearsals. A man's character is evidenced by everything he does and how he does it. . . . This, in a nutshell, was his 'method of physical action'—the ultimate in Stanislavski's system." Nevertheless, though it is true that this may have been Stanislavski's final word, it would seem to have been so only because death prevented him from adding others. To this, Kedrov also agreed in our conversation, and he reminded me that Komissarzhevski, when he attended the master's last rehearsal a month before his death, heard Stanislavski say emphatically, " 'I don't want to die . . . I feel that I am only beginning to understand things in the theatre, that I am only at the beginning of my road.' "

The Art Theatre has, according to Kedrov, sought to keep its master's flexibility of approach, and to continue to make improvements on Stanislavski's system. But the results do not seem to bear witness to much success. For the truth of the matter is that MXAT performances today are lack-luster affairs devoid of taste on the one hand and of conviction on the other. The only breathtakingly brilliant performances I witnessed were of *Dead Souls* and *The Three Sisters*. The former was the work of Stanislavski himself, who continues to get program credit for its staging. Chichikov, the hero-villain of the piece, is superbly performed by Belokyrov; he is the epitome of hypocrisy and obsequiousness. There are superb vignettes created by Stanitsin as the Governor, and by Kedrov, Gribov, and Livanov, all of whom (with the possible exception of Belokyrov) were part of the original cast when Stanislavski staged it thirty years ago. This, in other words, is the

Old Guard, and they have not forgotten the secrets they learned.

The Three Sisters, on the other hand, owes much of the lyrical beauty of its restaged production and its delicate sense of vulnerability to the youthfulness of the girls who play the Prozorov sisters and Natasha, and to the boy who plays Andrei. All of them are still in their twenties, which is a considerable improvement over the rather antediluvian casts one all too frequently sees in this play when it is presented professionally in the West.

Among the other productions which I saw at the Art Theatre—all of them added to the repertoire since the founders' deaths—none had the power to lift me out of myself as I had been moved in the old days. Of course, I may have changed along with the MXAT, and possibly it takes more to excite me than it did twenty-five years ago! Yet *A Winter's Tale* seemed heavy, tasteless, and without charm or poetry. *The Brothers Karamazov* was marred by a quite aging, moth-eaten Dmitri, although the character should be presented as the epitome of reckless and spirited youth. *The Sea Gull* seemed to convey none of the pulsing longings and frustrations (and little of the humor) that I know it possesses; and the performance of the great Alla Tarasova as Arkadina was particularly mechanical. Lillian Hellman's *The Autumn Garden,* which was hailed in New York as "Chekhovian," should by all rights have been given a sensitive performance at Chekhov's home base; but the result was an uneasily comic melodrama full of caricatured "types." Even the Ministry of Culture urged me not to see the MXAT's rendition of *Death of a Salesman* because it was considered so disappointing. And so it went.

There is no substitute for genius. That is what the Moscow Art Theatre had in abundance during its first thirty years. It cannot really be blamed, I suppose, if it is unable to come up with more geniuses. But the famous aquamarine-and-white-faced structure on the street that has now been named for it houses other problems for which it can indeed be blamed.

In my previous book, *Moscow Rehearsals,* I entitled the chapter that dealt with the Art Theatre "Actors at Work," for my contention was that it was a theatre in which the actor was paramount. I made this distinction between it and the theatres of Meierhold and Tairov because I was of the opinion that the latter two existed principally for the sake of their directors. While in retrospect I believe this distinction was justified, I think a postscriptural remark must now be made. The MXAT was much more a director's theatre than I realized or, I think, than *it* did.

Stanislavski always contended that the director's function was only to help the actor, and his modesty persuaded us to believe this was true. However, once he and Nemirovich-Danchenko were gone, it became clear how very much the MXAT had depended on their dynamic leadership. Russians are prone to hero worship: From Lenin to Van Cliburn we have evidence of it. The Art Theatre depended on its two founders as children depend on strict but loving parents. Deprived of them, their offspring felt lost. The trouble was that no one person could acceptably assume the patriarchal role. The most nearly acceptable was Nikolai Khmelyov, and he unfortunately died in 1945.

Today, the Moscow Art Theatre is run by a colloquium, or council of ten people. Mikhail Kedrov is its chairman. Alla Tarasova represents the acting company, Boris Livanov and Pavel Markov the literary side. In addition, there are the heads of the scenic, technical, and casting departments and of the business administration. All major decisions are made by this group. Now, I know that this is the accepted Soviet way of collective governing, but I fear it is not an adequate sub-

stitute for the autocratic authority of a Stanislavski-Nemir-
ovich partnership. Today, as a result, no one director places
the theatre's stamp on its productions. Even when Nemirovich and Stanislavski were trying to shift their power to
younger shoulders, each was finally responsible for his half
of the production schedule and each took a strong part in
shaping the final product on which a younger *régisseur* may
indeed have done most of the work. But, today, observe the
number of directors credited with the current MXAT repertoire:*

V. Y. Stanitsin	*Mary Stuart, The Cherry Orchard, Battle along the Road*
I. M. Raevski ⎫ N. N. Litovsev ⎬	*The Three Sisters, The Sea Gull*
B. N. Livanov ⎫ P. A. Markov ⎬ B. B. Markov ⎭	*The Brothers Karamazov*
M. N. Kedrov	*The Third Pathetique, A Winter's Tale, Uncle Vanya*
G. G. Konski	*The Blue Bird* (current revival), *The Devil's Disciple*
A. M. Karev	*Death of a Salesman, Jupiter Laughs, Everything Belongs to the People*
P. V. Leslie	*The Fox and the Grapes, A Nest of Gentlefolk*
I. M. Tarkhanov	*A Doll's House*
V. K. Monukov	*Battle along the Road, The Road Through Sokolniki*
S. K. Blinnikov	*The Smug Citizens*
E. M. Golisheva ⎫ B. R. Irakov ⎬	*The Autumn Garden*
M. M. Yanshin	*A Nest of Gentlefolk*

* The current productions of *Dead Souls, The Lower Depths,* and *Kremlin Chimes* are omitted, since they pre-date the deaths of both Stanislavski and Nemirovich-Danchenko.

If ever too many cooks were spoiling the broth, it would seem to be at the MXAT. How can this theatre hope to reassert its own personality when sixteen *régisseurs* are all asserting themselves, sometimes two and three of them in one production? I am familiar with this criticism, for the Phoenix Theatre in New York faced it regularly from its second through its sixth season, during my co-managing directorship; but the Phoenix in that period was striving for exactly the opposite aim from that of the Moscow theatres: It sought variety rather than homogeneity.

In addition to weak and diffuse leadership, the Moscow Art Theatre also suffers today from another result of Stanislavski's death: the lack of a middle generation. My attention was first called to this fact by one of Moscow's most discerning drama critics, Alexander Karaganov, and my own reaction upholds his judgment. I have expressed unqualified enthusiasm only for *Dead Souls,* in which the older generation, playing like a great orchestra, emanated such brilliance; and for *The Three Sisters,* in which the dominant impression evoked was one of youth. But in most plays on any stage the burden must be borne neither by the juveniles and ingénues nor by the old character actors, so that a theatre without a middle generation of leading men and women is bound to be out of joint. The root of the trouble lies in the fact that the older generation of the MXAT did not retire soon enough. Let me cite one example. Olga Knipper-Chekhova, Chekhov's widow, played Mme Ranyevskaya in *The Cherry Orchard*— the role of a woman of forty—until she was seventy. Alla Tarasova, when she *was* forty, should have been playing the role. But by the time Tarasova succeeded to it, she was fifteen years too old.

I readily understand how this could have happened. In fact, the reason the MXAT seemed so great as late as 1935 was because that first generation still *did* play. Too old or not, they knew their roles backward; they had grown up in them, and they could convey every nuance of feeling and meaning with absolute authority. Why alter such a memorable state of affairs? The older generation today, who are in reality the second generation of the MXAT, are a band of talented artists who grew up in that theatre between 1917 and 1937; the younger generation are those who have been accepted into the company since 1957. In the two decades that followed Stanislavski's death, the MXAT appears to have drawn no great talent to it. I cannot mention a single extraordinary actor there today who is between the ages of thirty and fifty. That generation seems merely to have learned by rote from others.

The first significant change in the Moscow Art Theatre in the last quarter-century was due to the death of its co-directors. The second change has been due to the fact that, by government fiat, the MXAT has been forced into becoming a kind of Russian Comédie Française. It happened in this way.

In the middle of the thirties, the Party line established itself in favor of socialist realism. Stalin and his henchmen had arrived at the point where they looked upon any cultivation of artistic form for its own sake as a dereliction of the artist's responsibility, and hence "counterrevolutionary" to the extent that it divorced itself from interpreting the problems of society. They considered as meaningless anything which did not "represent" life, and they demanded that life be "reproduced" on the stage—but with this added qualification: that in this reproduction, man must be represented only as a social being. "Socialist realism which began as an attitude toward art," I observed in 1935, "thus ends up as a style of art."

The great exponent of realism was, of course, the MXAT;

so the Art Theatre became the one acceptable theatre. Shortly
after the première of *Anna Karenina* in the spring of 1937 (a
production that, incidentally, is no longer part of the MXAT
repertoire), the Moscow Art Theatre was awarded the Order
of Lenin, the highest honor at the disposal of the government.
Stanislavski, Nemirovich-Danchenko, Kachalov, Moskvin, and
Leonidov individually received the same award. Thus the
official stamp of approval was placed upon the MXAT, its
leaders, and the principles for which they stood. Simultaneously, or shortly thereafter, all those who had ventured to
take artistic issue with Stanislavski's theories, notably Meierhold and Tairov, were struck down. The only acceptable
orthodoxy was the MXAT and its realism. Everything else
became "deviationist," "formalistic," or "decadent."

In thus exalting the Art Theatre at the expense of all the
other theatres of Moscow, a blow was struck at the whole
spirit of experiment that had glowed so strongly in the first
two decades after the Revolution. But the one to suffer most
of all was, paradoxically, the MXAT itself. It is simply not
good to be told that you and you alone have the answer. You
are bound to become rigid, self-satisfied, uncompromising.
Indeed, you can hardly help becoming so, when the government is backing you to the full and calling all your neighbors
heretics.

Today, the MXAT is paying the penalty for this primacy.
When Stalinism itself became heretical after the Twentieth
Party Congress in 1956, the Art Theatre was left high and
dry. Cautiously, Meierhold (or rather his memory) was
vindicated; cautiously, theatres began to reassert themselves;
they no longer needed to be carbon copies of the MXAT.
The result has been a natural wave of antipathy toward the
Art Theatre. I think that a good deal of the disapproval of
it, which is expressed by discerning theatregoers today, stems
from the fact that they are fed up with realism and are at-

tracted to those theatres which offer a "new look." The MXAT's stance, which is much the one it has always taken, does not please the sophisticated.

And so the circle comes full turn. The theatre which began as revolutionary at the turn of the century, which was looked upon as reactionary by the early Revolutionists and as ideal by the Stalinists, is now, in Khrushchev's Russia, considered none of these things: It is just "old hat" and a little bit boring—and *that* in the theatre is the kiss of death.

In front of the Maly Theatre sits a great bronze likeness of Ostrovski, master of Russian realistic drama in the nineteenth century. If his name means less in the West than do the names of some of his contemporaries, it is perhaps because he was so deeply Russian. Consequently, if the Maly is less known in the West than the Moscow Art Theatre, it is probably because it, too, as the spiritual home of Ostrovski, is, so to speak, less cosmopolitan, more deeply Russian. Maly means small, and it derives its name from its contrast with the Bolshoi, its neighbor in time and place, whose name means large. Actually, the Maly is of average size for drama. But, in any case, many of Moscow's inhabitants have always cherished it as their city's most beloved theatre. There is, in fact, a strongly Russian look to the place the moment you enter. The MXAT's fin de siècle, art nouveau decor seems more European (old-fashioned though it is) than Slavic; and its restful color scheme of brown, gray, and sage green does not quite belong to Moscow. By contrast, everything about the Maly—its foyer with ultramarine walls set off by white columns and white and gold trim, its crystal chandeliers, the crimson damask of its auditorium combined again with white and gold, the Empire painted ceiling that has miraculously been undisturbed—conspires to make it look like a product of the Russia of Alexander I, whose Greek Revival style one sees preserved in all its neoclassical elegance in a dozen palaces and country houses and recreated on the stage in the settings for *The Queen of Spades, Eugene Onegin,* and *War and Peace.*

Today, Ostrovski no longer dominates the repertoire of the house over which his figure presides. During that last fortnight in October, 1960, which I have used to illustrate the Moscow Art Theatre's repertoire, only two of the seventeen plays presented by the Maly were those of Ostrovski. There were three other Russian classics: Tolstoi's *The Power of Darkness* and *The Living Corpse,* and Chekhov's *Ivanov;* two English classics: *Vanity Fair* and *Lady Windermere's Fan;* and there was a Finnish drama: *The Stone Nest.* The other nine plays were by Soviet authors. The Maly, therefore, seems more contemporary than its seventy-four-year-younger sister, the Art Theatre. In fact, it likes to think that it has overtaken the MXAT since the death of Stanislavski. I would, however, rank these two theatres approximately on a par with the Maly's newer productions being, if anything, more interesting than those of the Art Theatre.

Like all Russian theatres, the Maly has absorbed many of Stanislavski's teachings, especially after the director Ilya Sudakov came to it from the MXAT in 1937. I did find its performance of Chekhov's *Ivanov,* for instance, perhaps more broadly and forcefully played than I was accustomed to in the Art Theatre interpretation, nor was the same care taken to create individual portraits for the twenty or thirty extras who decorate the drawing room in the party scene: They simply stood awkwardly around the periphery, looking embarrassed. Yet otherwise, truth and freshness, humor and passion were mingled in a more effective blend than in the MXAT's current performances of either *The Cherry Orchard* or *The Sea Gull.*

I feel that some of the increased vigor in the Maly today

results from the infusion of new blood, of artists who lack the Maly tradition but compensate for it by having had different backgrounds. I have already mentioned Sudakov, who came from the MXAT. The theatre's Artistic Director, Mikhail Tsaryov, grew up in Meierhold's theatre; as did Igor Ilinski, who staged the Maly's *Vanity Fair* and who, through his performance, makes Akim, the old peasant father in *The Power of Darkness,* a figure of unforgettable grandeur. Both of these men came to the Maly when the theatre of Meierhold, their earlier master, was dissolved at the end of the thirties. In addition, other directors from outside the Maly tradition have been invited to come there to stage specific productions: Boris Ravenskikh directed *The Power of Darkness,* and the late Alexei Diki was also a guest *régisseur.* The most recent and antipodal director to receive an invitation from the Maly is Nikolai Okhlopkov.

As for the Maly acting company itself, I think the same criticism can be leveled against it as has been leveled against the MXAT. It has some fine old actors, some fine quite young actors, but few outstanding ones in between. This is possibly why Tsaryov, who must be in his sixties, plays—and excellently, I grant—the hero of *The Living Corpse,* a character twenty years younger than himself. On the other hand, we find admirable youngsters like Nikolai Podgorny, whose uncle was one of the Art Theatre's "greats," creating a whole gallery of admirably defined portraits that range from Borkin, the anxious estate manager in *Ivanov,* to the harried young Soviet student hero of O. N. Stukalov's *House of Cards,* which he plays "straight."

Is it a coincidence that the only two dramatic theatres of Moscow which receive governmental subsidies—the Maly and the Art Theatre—are the most conservative and academic? The answer one is given is, of course, that they are the two oldest, the two largest (the MXAT has one hundred and forty actors in its company and the Maly has one hundred and twenty), that they have two stages apiece to maintain, that they have the largest repertoires, and that their conservatism has nothing to do with their subvention. Perhaps all this is true. But one may be forgiven for wondering whether a long tradition of large government subsidy of a theatre (as is also the case of the Comédie Française) may not induce a certain stiffening of the joints and hardening of the arteries. It is perhaps good to have to fight for your livelihood.

One of the most newsworthy facts that I discovered on my trip is that today the government does not support all Moscow theatres. On the authority of Alexander N. Kuznetsov, Deputy Minister of Culture of the U.S.S.R., I can state that the Soviet government provides subsidies for only three theatres in Moscow: the Bolshoi opera and ballet company, and the two dramatic theatres just mentioned. Every other theatre in the city, as well as approximately ninety-nine out of a hundred of the Soviet Union's other five hundred and seventy-six theatres, has to earn its own living. This fact disproves the long-accepted assumption, which I, among others, have been guilty of perpetuating, to the effect that all the playhouses of the Soviet Union are underwritten by the government. In actual fact, though a theatre's losses are not made good by the government, its profits are siphoned off to the state. For, of course, all theatres are state-owned, even if not state-supported.

Each theatre, it appears, must so budget its expenditures and must so juggle its repertoire to meet popular demand that it will end each season by at least breaking even. If it struggles through too many seasons with a deficit, either the management is overhauled or the company is closed down. It is fortunate for the country's legitimate theatre that there is an insatiable demand for almost anything theatrical. If this should ever change, Soviet Russia's theatres, competing for a dwindling public, might, improbable though it seems, end up looking unedifyingly like the commercial theatres of Broadway, for whom a healthy box office is the only talisman of success.

5

New Blood in
the Theatre

Moscow is not very different from other large cities. It is really a collection of small communities, each one possessing a consanguinity of interest and occupation. Established theatre people in New York all know each other or know about each other. In London, the same, I find, holds true. In Moscow, because it is smaller than either of the other two capitals, everybody seems to know even more about everybody else's business. For the researcher, this is a happy situation, for, once he establishes connections, it is not very hard to get everyone's impressions of everyone else.

That is how I know that the Sovremennik* group was the most talked of company in Moscow at the beginning of the sixties, and that it is the company most generally encouraged by all in the profession. For I had been in Moscow not more

---

* Sovremennik is the masculine noun derived from the adjective sovremenny, meaning modern or contemporary. The contemporary man is a proper translation.

than a week before I was told that the creation of the Sovremennik was the most newsworthy event of the past few years.
"You *must* see the Sovremennik," said Lydia Kislova, one
of the heads, at that time, of the Society for Friendship and
Cultural Relations with Foreign Countries (and a charming,
motherly woman not nearly as formidable as the title of her
organization). So, too, said one of the Deputy Ministers of
Culture. A prominent drama critic reiterated the advice, as
did also the American cultural attaché and the directors of
the Mayakovski and Vakhtangov theatres. Whatever it was,
it became clear to me that this organization was on everybody's mind.

But it is one thing to be told you must see the Sovremennik
and another thing to accomplish it. For in September and
October, 1960, no performances were announced. No building to which one could go and inquire bore its name. And
one could not find the theatre listed in the telephone direc-
tory, for the very good reason that there are no directories
to be got hold of in Moscow.*

Finally, Mikhail Kedrov remarked a month after I had
arrived, "If you want to meet the Sovremennik people,
nothing could be easier. They are rehearsing just across the
way. I've this minute left them to keep my appointment with
you." He rose and looked out the window of the MXAT
office. "Those are their windows just opposite," he said. "I'll
phone across and ask their director to come over and say
hello. Then you can make an appointment with him. The
Sovremennik people are all old students of mine." A few
minutes later young Oleg Yefremov answered the summons.
Slender, fair-haired, with bright, amused eyes that darted
quickly in every direction, he grasped my hand firmly and

---

* This is one of those Soviet paradoxes. There are plenty of automatic dial
phones, but no way of finding out people's numbers. Everyone in Moscow has,
in effect, a private listing!

smiled. "Come and see us whenever you like," he said. "We rehearse every day at eleven."

Three days later I pulled the proffered latchstring and found myself in the Sovremennik rehearsal room. On the walls hung portraits of three of the Moscow Art Theatre's great original company: Kachalov, Moskvin, and Leonidov. They were enlarged photographs, taken probably thirty-five years ago, and the old-fashioned collars and pince-nez made them seem very much a part of the past. The room was a little pool of quiet concentration on which the old triumvirate looked down noncommittally from their frames. A dozen young people were seated in a circle around a little table, behind which sat Yefremov. They were about to start reading a new script, a Czech play based on the old fairy-tale story of *The Three Wishes,* but laid in modern times. No one appeared to be more than thirty (I learned later that the eldest, Yefremov himself, was thirty-three), and there were more young men than girls in the circle. Most of the men were wearing sports shirts and the girls were wearing pullover sweaters. There was an air of easy camaraderie and mutual respect that was readily perceptible.

I thought back to my first year in the professional theatre—to the University Players on Cape Cod—in the days when, like me, Henry Fonda, Margaret Sullavan, James Stewart, Joshua Logan, and a couple of dozen others were beginning to try their wings. Perhaps these memories and the similarity between these young Russians and the University Players made me feel an immediate rapport with them. As I came to know them better, it seemed to me the resemblance grew more striking, except that we had failed to accomplish our group objective, whereas, I suspect, they may succeed.

To the farewell call I had made on Stanislavski in 1935, I had taken with me a clipping from a New York newspaper, and which I had read to him. The clipping told of the anticipated re-creation of our University Players, which had disbanded early in the depression. In order, I believe, to distinguish this group's point of view from that of the Group Theatre, the other young American theatre organization of the 1930's—a group which had positive political and esthetic principles which it widely publicized—this press release about the University Players had said that we had "no political, social, or artistic credo to promote: it only wants to present good plays well done." When I had finished reading the clipping, Stanislavski had taken off his glasses and, twirling them by their black ribbon, had said, "I think such a statement is meaningless. Everybody wants to present good plays well done. I have never heard of anyone who made it his aim to present bad plays badly. That is no basis on which to create a theatre." He had paused, then leaned forward, and continued. "When Nemirovich and I founded our theatre, we were in revolt against the prevailing practices of the time. It is always necessary to be in revolt in order to create. You must be dissatisfied with things as they are. You must want to change them. That's what creation means: Something is made that did not exist before. If you only want to go on as others have done before you, you are an imitator, not a creator. Some people are capable only of imitation, I grant, but surely you don't want to start a theatre with that as your goal."

The young people who founded the Sovremennik could hardly have heard these words from Stanislavski's own lips, for the eldest was but nine years old when Stanislavski died. But they understood his meaning. That was precisely why they had not wanted to be absorbed into the MXAT when they graduated. To do that meant going on in the ways of their forefathers. It meant waiting perhaps twenty years until the older generation had passed from the scene. By that time, they would have been in the groove themselves, their creative energy spent. They would have learned to live with their present dissatisfactions until they no longer seemed to exist. No, they must get out and start something new. They must create!

Yet the Soviet Union is probably the most difficult place in the world for young people to do just this. In England or America, the only thing a person has to do to start a theatre, or any business enterprise for that matter, is to start it. I know, for I have done it. And this is not to say that there are not a thousand obstacles in the way. Yet, if you can find the means of overcoming the problems, you can have your theatre, and no one will stop you. But a planned society has no room for the maverick. In it, a man cannot undertake a project on his own initiative, simply because he thinks it is a good idea. The Russian stands ready to serve the omniscient Party: It is the Party that initiates new ideas.

This is the reason, I suspect, that every Muscovite's hat is off to the Sovremennik youngsters. They have accomplished the impossible simply by the very act of creating a theatre or, rather, by persuading the government to let them do so. Even if their theatre were to be dissolved by the time these words are printed, they will have made their point. The history of the Soviet theatre during the first dozen years after the Revolution is full of examples of mushrooming groups. Stanislavski was always sympathetic to young people who wanted to strike out on their own; the MXAT sponsored four studios, beginning with one which—created by Leopold Sulerzhitski, Michael Chekhov, and Vakhtangov—subsequently became the Second Moscow Art Theatre, now dissolved. But I think I am right in saying that, while other theatres have changed personnel and sometimes even their names, the Sovremennik is the first Moscow theatre to come into existence from scratch in more than twenty years.

The time was propitious. A new wind was blowing after 1956. There was a popular wave of boredom with the MXAT which these youngsters rode. The new Minister of Culture, Yekaterina Furtseva, was sympathetic to fresh ideas and had tremendous power to wield in behalf of the ideas and the people who interested her. So it was that in 1957 the Sovremennik Theatre came into being, haltingly at first, in full form a year later. The theatre was about to begin its third season in the autumn of 1960 when I first crossed its path.

"Each generation needs to find its own way," one of the young actors explained, when a pause came in the reading and they clustered around their guest. "Most of us felt that the MXAT, in whose school we were trained, was not interpreting life the way we saw it, so we could not be happy becoming part of that company, much as we respected and loved it. We could not accept what we were told. We had to find out for ourselves."

The break, one suspects, was painful, the more so for their mentors than for themselves, for there are intimations that the older generation was not happy, as Stanislavski seems always wisely to have been, when the fledglings left the nest. The older ones apparently felt a little like the late Queen Mary when her son abdicated the throne from which she expected to see him rule. Nevertheless, the parent MXAT has accepted the situation with as good grace as possible. It has been of help in providing rehearsal space, its filial stage for occasional performances, and a certain amount of moral support.

The Sovremennik's principal assistance, however, comes from the Ministry of Culture itself, which views it with a fairly indulgent, paternalistic eye. Its program carries the line, "Ministry of Culture of the U.S.S.R." above the words Sovremennik Studio Theatre. The relationship of the Ministry to this theatre is thus formally recognized, though it is not spelled out. The theatre claims that in reality the government has, after providing a small grant to set it up in busi-

ness, so to speak, given it "not a kopek," and that it has been
sink or swim ever since. The Ministry explains its feeling of
responsibility for the Sovremennik on the grounds that, since
the Moscow Art Theatre is under its direct jurisdiction, so
must be this offshoot of the MXAT.

One great problem for these young people in starting a
theatre was that of finding a home. The Sovremennik began
without a building in sight; just a group of actors, a dynamic
leader, and an idea. Three years later, when I was in Moscow, they were still without a home, although, in the spring
of 1961, they finally fell heir to the Variety Theatre on
Mayakovski Square. Prior to that good fortune, they presented their performances in the large concert hall of the
Sovietskaya Hotel; but there were many other programs taking place in this hall, and thus Sovremennik performances
had to be sandwiched into a tight schedule of bookings with
woefully little time to set up scenery and lights. It became
an even more critical problem when the theatre had a new
production to mount, with dress rehearsals, previews, and
all the accompanying complications. The hall, which seats
about seven hundred, has both an adequate stage and a com-
fortable auditorium, but it is quite a long distance from the
center of town and it always seemed like transient lodgings,
failing to exude the special aura provided by all the other
Moscow theatre buildings for their companies. Yet, in less
than three years the Sovremennik had already built up an enthusiastic following; at the time I was there they never had
an empty seat; they were able to pay their bills and support
themselves out of box-office savings through the lean months
when there was no place for them to play. They will, I am
convinced, survive successfully and, in another decade, they
will probably be one of the most important of Moscow's
theatres.

Who are these people and what are their ideas? The answer to the first question is quickly found. They are a collective of twenty-five young actors, all but five of whom are graduates of the Nemirovich-Danchenko Theatre School of the MXAT (the others having graduated from the schools attached to the Maly and the Vakhtangov). None of them is very famous. Some came straight from school into this company. The older ones worked elsewhere for a few years before coming together to form the Sovremennik. Yefremov worked as actor and director at the Central Children's Theatre; Mikhail Kazakov, one of the principal actors, has made a number of motion pictures and had played the title role in *Hamlet* at the Mayakovski. Seven of the original group had at the time of my visit weathered the entire three years. The others—like Kazakov—had left whatever they were doing to join this troupe of their contemporaries.

"Khrushchev's great hope, the Soviet Union's great hope, lies in the young—those under thirty-five," Edward Crankshaw, the London *Observer's* distinguished Russian analyst, has asserted in his recent book, *Khrushchev's Russia*. "The best of these, and there are many who are very good by any standards, inhabit a world of their own which has every appearance of being utterly removed from the world of their elders." I doubt that Mr. Crankshaw knew of these Sovremennik youngsters, but it is they and their ilk that he describes when he speaks of the "well-turned-out young men in their thirties, usually Party members, relaxed and easy in manner, often with a pleasantly ironical approach to life, and very much in touch with realities of every kind—understanding, moreover, a great deal more about the realities of life outside the Soviet Union than they usually allow to be known, and no less of the gulf between Kremlin pretensions and Kremlin practice. These confident and unfrightened young men are springing up like grass." Their theatre is the Sovremennik. That is why it carries such importance.

What kind of theatre do these young people want to create? They have two objectives. First, they want a theatre for actors. They feel that in today's Moscow most theatres are dominated by the director, who imposes his ideas and his style upon the performers. Both Yefremov and Yevgeny Yevstigneyev, who share most of the direction at the Sovremennik, began as actors, and they propose continuing to perform. I must say I am dubious about how this will work out, for inevitably the strongest personalities will dominate (it is happening already) and, inevitably, they will mold the company in their own image. However, if the intent remains firm to keep this a collective enterprise, albeit under strong leadership—even as the MXAT and the Vakhtangov were in their early days—my doubts may prove groundless.

The Sovremennik's second objective relates to repertoire. So far, the group has tackled no classics, and this is as they wish it. ("Later, when we are ready," they say.) The life of today, the problems of their generation honestly presented— these are things with which they want to come to grips, and this is doubtless why Victor Rozov attracted them and they him. For the opening of their theatre, Rozov gave them his *The Immortal Ones*, a play on which his world-renowned film, *The Cranes Are Flying*, is based. The drama goes back to World War II for its action, but the conflict between the opportunistic and the selfless individual is still pertinent, as was evident from the Sovremennik production which I saw at a dress rehearsal of its revival. The wartime atmosphere was established by means of antiaircraft searchlights, which combed the night sky above the ceilingless room. An "eternal flame," glowing high above the stage, added patriotic symbolism in keeping with the title. Yet the actors simultaneously established an immediacy in relation to the action that made the play speak not as history but as of contemporary life. The acting was in muted key. Sometimes passages were not altogether audible (a fact forgivable, in my opinion, only because this was a dress rehearsal); but there was that truth to life that we associate with the disciples of Stanislavski, and, on the basis of this production, I concluded that the Sovremennik acting style did not actually conflict with the basic tenets of the MXAT.

One of the problems that besets any young company is how to portray older characters convincingly. This, I recall, was one of the University Players' chief difficulties. For the Sovremennik actors, however, there appears to be no such hurdle to surmount. They are altogether capable of upping their ages twenty to forty years, as the play requires, without ever making one feel that beneath the wrinkles laid on with grease paint there is a boy's face or that the grandmother is only a girl beneath powdered hair.

"When you see the performances of the Sovremennik, a young theatre just hatched," wrote Nikolai Ophlopkov in a recent article in the Soviet magazine, *Teatr,* "you are charmed in spite of the immaturity of most of the actors. These gifted youngsters draw the audience into the action; they leave the doors open for the imagination to enter. They act truthfully and sincerely—but this is not naturalism."

I agree with Okhlopkov.

My other opportunity to see the Sovremennik in action came when they gave a single performance of Yevgeny Schwarz's *The Naked King.* Unfortunately, the young troupe was not altogether at ease in fantasy. Effects were somewhat too broadly achieved; the actors had to "reach" for laughs. Yet the production's modest decor (consisting of two little turntables with a set piece on each, which the actors turned around in full view of the audience); its bright costumes, which had a distinctly improvised, rag-bag look about them; its heavily stylized make-ups, which made every character look preposterously old or sanguine or pallid, virginal or vil-

lainous—all these blended to make a gay and cheerful, if not
subtle, impression. The play, I suspect, needs more irony,
more edge, in its playing, but the significant thing about this
presentation was that the Sovremennik had the nerve to do
it at all. It is the only theatre where any work of the brilliant
but seldom heard satirist is played in Moscow today. Rumor
had it that, as a matter of fact, the version I saw was an ex-
purgated one and not the full text as first staged.

On one hand, I mark this production as bold. On the other
hand, I note this particular group's expressed disapproval of
such a play as Arbuzov's widely adored *An Irkutsk Story*. Of
the Arbuzov drama, one Sovremennik actor told me, "It's just
sentimental claptrap; that's not what *we* mean by dealing
with the problems of our time." The conclusion I draw is
that this group has a mind of its own and is not prepared to
swallow a line dished out to it.

Do not infer anything political from this attitude. The fact
is that the younger generation is committed to communism
and to the Soviet state. But they are not the dewy-eyed romantic idealists of the twenties and the thirties. They are
not taken in by slogans nor, I suspect, by the general propaganda output. They are ready to ask embarrassing questions
and to speak their own minds. They are critical of the weaknesses of the Soviet regime and the inadequacies of their way
of life. Yet they do not want to overthrow the government;
they merely want to improve it. I would be guilty of a kind
of Joe McCarthy injustice if I accused them of being subversive just because they are honest. If the government closes
the Sovremennik, the world can take note that it is afraid of
the group. But at this point the government is allowing them
to speak, and it is a good thing for all concerned. For, as
Edward Crankshaw has made clear, the "success or failure of
Khrushchev as a reforming statesman will depend in the end
on whether he can win [the younger generation's] confidence,

establishing a direct link between himself and the younger generations, by-passing in effect what I have called the lost generation . . ."

As I listened to these young people talk about their desire to create an epoch-making theatre, I could not help but compare them with today's youth in the American theatre. A decade ago such a comparison would have been all to our disadvantage. Few of our young people were prepared at the beginning of the 1950's to start out on their own. Security was the watchword, although how anyone ever thought he would find it in the theatre, heaven knows. But in the last ten years, the tone has changed. We have seen José Quintero gather a series of such hitherto unheard-of young actors as Geraldine Page, Jason Robards, Jr., George C. Scott, and Colleen Dewhurst; take over an unused night club; and create a "Circle in the Square." We have seen Joseph Papp force the powerful Park Commissioner of the City of New York into continuing and, indeed, expanding his free Shakespeare Festivals in Central Park. We have seen a group of young actors calling themselves the Association of Producing Artists—led by Ellis Rabb and Rosemary Harris—start down a path extraordinarily like the Sovremennik's, with no theatre, just a company and an idea. We have seen the off-Broadway movement grow from two or three pioneering groups to a conglomerate of thirty or more playhouses presenting more than twice as many productions as did Broadway in the 1960–1961 season—and most of it done by what could be called the younger generation. Farther afield, the last decade has seen young Tom Patterson create the Stratford Shakespearean Festival Theatre in Ontario in the face of desperate odds. It has witnessed university students in Minnesota and Indiana piloting showboats up and down the Mississippi and Ohio rivers. It has seen young people in San Francisco establish a resident professional acting company. If the Sovremennik

Theatre chartered a plane and flew to the United States, it would discover a great many of its American contemporaries caught up in the same dream and wrestling with many of the same problems.

What differences, apart from political ideology, would there be? First, of course, the Sovremennik group has the advantage in technical training. Its members know what they are doing, for they have had four years' schooling; they know how to play a sixty-year-old man and how to look that age, for they have been taught how to do so. Secondly, the Russians are grounded in a tradition—in their case the Moscow Art Theatre's—which our young people lack. They speak a common artistic language which is, in a sense, part of their MXAT birthright. Even conceding a common background, which is rarely possible in our country, their American contemporaries have no such language to learn. The Sovremennik group and one of our own might have this in common: that each knows better what it is against than what it is for. Yet, I feel that although the Sovremennik has still to define clearly its artistic line, it will do so, now that its leaders have time to think about things other than where the next performance is to take place or where the next ruble is coming from, whereas most of our young people do not even know what is meant by an artistic line. All these American enterprises have a transient air to them (except for San Francisco's Actors' Workshop and Canada's Stratford). Most of them seem to be a means to an end. Perhaps I feel this way because the history of the American theatre contains a series of similar undertakings that have flourished and then faded, as their leaders and participants have become discouraged through failure or, conversely, have moved through success to something more lucrative and personally aggrandizing. But the Sovremennik gives the impression that it is here to stay. This may be because I see all around it theatres that *have* stayed, not for a few bright seasons but for decades. It is even possible that the Stanislavski tradition rests more securely in the hands of the Sovremennik group than it does at the Art Theatre itself. At the Art Theatre the tradition maintains itself by ritual, by patriarchs who look backward. At the Sovremennik it is being carried forward by acolytes who look into the future.

6

The Meierhold

Tradition

His "adventure into art has been solitary; when he is gone there will be no one to succeed him. His contribution was that of providing the impetus to theatrical revolution, and it is a contribution which has been completed. The influence of his style will certainly continue and perhaps in expressions more adequate to the needs of a proletariat whom he may have represented but one of whom he never was."

I wrote these words about Vsevolod Meierhold in 1935. By 1960, my prognostication had come true.

Meierhold lived through the most exciting period of the Soviet theatre, that of 1920 to 1935. Indeed, it was in large measure an exciting period for the very reason that he was there. I never really understood him; his esthetic aims were not mine. Yet there was a vividness in his theatrical genius, a fertility in his imagination, a scope in his mastery; and he was a superb actor, musician, designer, and *régisseur*. But he was not, as Robert Bolt said of Sir Thomas More, "a man for all seasons."

The Russian theatre emerged from the agony of the first years of the October Revolution in need of a new direction, new forms of expression, a new voice that would speak to a new audience. At that time the artists of the Moscow Art Theatre and of the Maly represented the bourgeois intelligentsia; they spoke with the quiet voice of the past; their realism was the expression in art of Capitalist materialism; or so it seemed to the fiery idealists who were forging a new society and wanted a theatre that would shout for the new day, that would fire the revolutionary spirit, that would smash traditions on the stage even as they had been smashed in society.

And so, under Meierhold, the Revolution surged into the theatre, ripping down the proscenium curtain, tumbling outrageously over the footlights, shocking the senses with speed and color and caricature. Paradoxically, Meierhold had turned to the past for his new forms. The theatre he was rebelling against had been dominant for only sixty years: It was the theatre that Ibsen, Zola, and Hauptmann had converted to their social ends through the use of realism, and in Meierhold's thinking they had brought a ponderous earnestness and a literal explicitness to playmaking, for which he had no use. So he reached back to the commedia dell'arte, to the Oriental and medieval theatres, to the marionette stage, to the Greeks, rolling these together and compounding the result by adding the constructivist, symbolist, abstractionist tendencies of the first two decades of the twentieth century. His work paralleled and was part of the same avant-garde flowering to which the Russians, Andrei Bely, Mikhail Zoshchenko, Isaac Babel, Vladimir Mayakovski, and Boris Pasternak were contributing in literature.

Meierhold was a revolution by himself. He was its spirit

and its substance and its great irony, too, for in 1939 he was
called before the bar of judgment to answer charges of counterrevolutionary "formalism." That Artists' Congress comes
down to us now as a memorable event. It was Meierhold's
last public appearance. In that meeting he is reported to have
stood up and made this searing speech:

The pitiful and wretched thing that pretends to the title of the
theatre of socialist realism has nothing in common with art.

But the theatre is art! And without art, there is no theatre! Go
visiting the theatres of Moscow. Look at their drab and boring
presentations that resemble one another and are each worse than
the others. . . . Recently creative ideas poured from them. People
in the arts searched, erred, and frequently stumbled and turned
aside, but they really created—sometimes badly and sometimes
splendidly. Where once there were the best theatres of the world,
now . . . everything is gloomily well-regulated, averagely arith-
metical, stupefying, and murderous in its lack of talent. Is that
your aim? If it is—oh!—you have done something monstrous! . . .
In hunting formalism, you have eliminated art!

Shortly thereafter, he himself disappeared and his wife was
found murdered. His theatre was closed. He is presumed to
have died in exile or in a concentration camp, and the name
of Vsevolod Meierhold became anathema.

How was I able to say just four years before he made this
great plea that his was a "contribution which has been completed"? The answer, I believe, lies in an understanding
of the way the artist is and has always been affected by materialism. Realism becomes dominant in art, it seems to me,
only at such times and in such places as man assumes that the
tangible is more important than the intangible. The history
of art reflects the history of man, and both reveal the swings
of the pendulum between the world and the spirit. As an-

cient Greece grew old, material concerns threw her earlier astonishing equilibrium out of balance. A Hellenistic art which was more "realistic" followed that idealization of man which the earlier Hellenic art had expressed so exquisitely. Rome, still more materialistic than Greece, expressed itself in even greater realism.

The Middle Ages and the Renaissance repeated the contrast: Medieval man, living an intensely spiritual life, turned to symbols in art that could express his mysticism. The great gold mosaics of Santa Sophia, the glass of Chartres, the portal of Notre Dame de Paris, the texts of *The Divine Comedy* and of *Everyman*—all these translated into art man's disregard for his material surroundings and his preoccupation with the life of the spirit.

As man next swung from the hereafter to the here, from things not seen to things seen, art swung with him, and the humanism of the Renaissance followed. But because those great centuries allied spirit with matter, realism in art was tempered, or expanded, by idealism. Both are blended in Shakespeare. As the eighteenth and nineteenth centuries drew man farther and farther away from intangibles and into a world dominated by industry and science—that is to say, into a social structure that was oriented materially—man's art became once again more and more committed to realism.

To all oversimplifications, such as the one in which I have just indulged, there are exceptions. But the history of Russian art helps to support my generalization. Until almost the very brink of our century, Russia as a whole lived in the Middle Ages. Her church was medieval, her society feudal. Her art, therefore, naturally continued to be liturgical and symbolic. Even when such great writers as Tolstoi and Dostoyevski arrived, they amazed a Western world that had forgotten the spirit, for they infused such mysticism into their view of life as had not been seen—save in such exceptional figures as Donne, Blake, and a few others—since before the Renaissance.

The early Revolutionists—the men who engineered the Revolution of 1905 and the intellectuals who supported them —were determined to break the mysticism that held Russia spiritually in thrall. To accomplish their social and political aims, they had to force their contemporaries to see that the world was capable of materialistic interpretation; Marx was, of course, the man for them. In art, realism became the appropriate medium to express their concern for the "facts" of life. Thus it was that the MXAT and the Maly were considered the two forward-looking, revolutionary theatres in the light of their productions of the late nineteenth- and early twentieth-century realists, Ostrovski and Ibsen, Chekhov, Hauptmann, and that really Revolutionary writer, Maxim Gorki.

Then came 1917. In the convulsions of the early years of the Revolution, the material ends were obscured. Since famine, disease, poverty, civil war, and internal violence of every kind consumed those years, life on this earth was very nearly unbearable. Lenin and others quickly realized that the people must return to the intangibles; the Revolution must become a kind of holy crusade. The ecstasy of the dream— now the dream of an ideal Socialist society—must imbue the people with a superhuman fervor, or the entire massive undertaking would collapse. During this period, when the challenge of communism was spiritual because it had no tangible gains to offer, the theatre that was needed was consequently an anti-realistic, almost poetic one—the theatre, in a word, of Mayakovski and Meierhold.

Once the agony of the first upheaval had subsided, the temper of the Revolutionary movement soon reasserted its

basically materialistic outlook. After Stalin succeeded Lenin
and inaugurated the Five-Year Plans of the late 1920's and
the 1930's, the eyes of the country were focused on material
objectives, on translating the fervor of the dream into the
realities of heavy industry, of better factories and farms, of
war material, of building, and of making things and still
more things.

And art? The pendulum swung back inevitably toward
realism and its preoccupation with the outwardly observable
fact. The Marxist interpretation of art had always been that
it must be a part of life, must express and be a weapon in
man's long struggle to "build socialism." Now, with the
liquidation of the aristocracy and of the bourgeoisie, art—
in this case the theatre—had to mirror the development of
the new man, to reflect his new life, which was now almost
completely concerned with material accomplishment. Realism was actually the only way in which this could be expressed effectively.

When a government is truly totalitarian, as is the Soviet,
it can, of course, determine the direction of every endeavor.
If it wants to abolish abstraction in each of the arts, calling
it decadent and "counterrevolutionary formalism," it can
do so. If it wants to say realism—"socialist realism"—is the
only acceptable form; it can do so. The man who cannot or
will not abide by the government's dictum must go. And
that is the way it was by the middle of the thirties. That is
why it was clear to anyone who understood the temper of
the Soviet times and the temper of Vsevolod Meierhold that
he was finished by 1935. Socialist realism stood for everything he abhorred. As an artist of inflexible integrity, he re-
fused to accept and to practice it. If he had not been a
great artist, it would not have mattered so much; but he
was, and so, like Pasternak two decades later, he had to be

sacrificed. With the one great dissenter silenced, socialist realism could sweep over the whole Soviet stage unchallenged. And it did, with cataclysmic results.

In 1959, the third year of the Khrushchev dispensation, a book by Victor Komissarzhevski, entitled *Moscow Theatres,* was published. It contains a picture of Meierhold, as well as photographs of three of his productions, *The Last Decisive, The Inspector-General,* and *Woe to Wit.* We are told therein that "producers and actors alike are making a careful study of Meierhold's work," for it is admitted that, "alongside formalistic errors and delusions, Meierhold's performances were imbued with the realistic poetry of his unconventional theatre. In exaggerated symbols, unexpected poetic mises-en-scene, tense and satiated rhythms, and a dynamic approach, Meierhold's best works render the great ideas of the contemporary world."

Cautiously, the work of rehabilitating the position of the early leader of the Revolutionary theatre now proceeds. His name crops up constantly and unselfconsciously in private discussions in Moscow, in public lectures, in magazine articles. The stenographic record of his rehearsals and what can be found of his correspondence are being assembled for near-future publication. The men who, literally to save their own necks, were silent in 1939 are now able to speak up and acknowledge their debt to him. This debt, which his contemporaries and successors owe to Meierhold, essentially lies in the reminder to them—and to us, wherever we work on the stage—that the theatre is not life but art; that in making its statements about life or truth or mankind or whatever it be called, the theatre must never lose sight of the fact that it is first and foremost theatre; furthermore, that it must be governed by esthetic laws, and must not yield to political dictation. The Soviet theatre lay under the stifling blanket of strictly interpreted socialist realism for almost twenty years. It has begun to toss and turn and show signs of kicking off that blanket. But after twenty years, during which a generation has grown up that knew only the realism dictated by Party hacks, it is not easy to know just where to go. That is when the example of Meierhold's kind of theatre rises up to point a way. That is why it is possible at last to speak of a "Meierhold tradition" in Moscow.

I said in 1935 that no one would succeed Meierhold; but the man who has come nearest to inheriting his mantle is Nikolai Okhlopkov of the Mayakovski Theatre. He is, at any rate, senior articulator for that wing of the Soviet theatre that opposes the Moscow Art Theatre's brand of academic realism. It is important to distinguish his similarities and dissimilarities to the archpriest of the "theatre theatrical" for when I say Meierhold's mantle has fallen on him, I must be careful to explain just what that means.

First of all, Okhlopkov is somewhat temperamentally reminiscent of his master. He is a great personal showman— so was Meierhold. He is a dictatorial director—so was Meierhold. One often hears the Mayakovski Theatre, which he heads, called Okhlopkov's Theatre, for his personality completely dominates the place. There are other *régisseurs* there (his wife is one of them), but they are inconspicuous alongside their leader. He holds the spotlight.

Okhlopkov's personality has always been a dominating one. Twenty-five years ago I suspected that one reason there were so few capable actors in his Realistic Theatre was perhaps the same reason that Meierhold had so few: Okhlopkov's was a one-man show, and he was the one man. "His demands must be executed to the letter and his temper is impatient," I observed. *"Régie* first and acting afterwards."

I can make the same observation a quarter of a century later. His theatre makes its impact in terms of production,

not of individual performance. Any really good actor, I suspect, eventually leaves Okhlopkov for a stage that allows
him more chance for personal development and creativity.
Sooner or later he will be dissatisfied with being clay in the
hands of a potter, no matter how masterful. I am reminded
a little of the productions directed by Tyrone Guthrie. My
admiration for Guthrie's directorial genius is immense, but
the impression I usually take from his presentations is of his
staging rather than of any single actor's unique contribution.
I used to have the same reaction years ago to productions
directed by Orson Welles. It is an impression that presumably cannot be avoided when an intensely creative director is
at work. The same obtains in the case of Okhlopkov.

Okhlopkov is also like Meierhold in that he insists his
audience must not come seeking to abandon itself to illu-
sion. He offers no slice-of-life, peephole realism. He does
not place upon his stage a literal representation of environment: three-wall box settings hold no interest for him. In
Hamlet, for instance, the production scheme he worked out
with his constant collaborator-designer, Vadim Ryndin, is
said to have been drawn from Hamlet's remark that "Den-
mark is a prison." Elsinore is presented as a sort of Viking
dungeon. This time the production is entirely contained
within the conventional proscenium, though this is not
Okhlopkov's usual custom. The stage is filled by two immense, solid lead, studded gates. Nevertheless, some scenes are
played on a forestage in front of the gates, and at times the
gates swing open to reveal a vast throne room, a glimpse of
seacoast, a graveyard; at other times, sections of these gates
rise like portcullises to show chambers or passages that seem
to honeycomb the castle like prison cells. Okhlopkov does
not ask the spectator to believe that Elsinore actually looked
like this; nor even that the play was performed in this way
in Shakespeare's theatre. He has established his own esthetic

frame of reference, and everything—the sound of trumpets, trombones, and drums; the heavy costumes, the nonillusionistic lighting—contributes to that ironclad frame. When Okhlopkov produces a play of contemporary life, like Alexander Stein's *Spring Violins,* he again does not ask the audience to accept the setting literally—the delicate shimmering aluminum tracery that outlines the Moscow skyline in the background, the silvery rods that define the façade of foreground apartment houses. He is working only to create a theatrical effect, just as the bright aquamarine sidewalk that cuts diagonally across the auditorium at the level of the stage is invented to enhance such an effect.

To remind the world that this theatricality is a line he has pursued since his beginnings in the theatre nearly forty years ago, Okhlopkov recently revived his production of Pogodin's *Aristocrats,* which I watched in rehearsals in 1935 and saw in performance in 1937. I went again in 1960 to see what changes might have been effected. I found none, save that the conventionality of his present playhouse makes for an awkwardness not necessitated by the theatre without proscenium in Krasnaya Presnaya. This realistically conceived story of the building of the White Sea canal by political prisoners, whose social rehabilitation is accomplished in the process, was given a treatment by Okhlopkov in 1935 that was most reminiscent of a Meierhold experiment: a stylized blending of elements taken principally from the commedia dell'arte and the Chinese theatre. There was no scenery nor were there any properties on the two bare rectangular platforms placed at angles to each other. In 1935, the platforms had occupied the center of the hall, with the upper left-hand corner of one connecting with the lower right-hand corner of the other. Now, in 1960, the two platforms spanned the orchestra pit diagonally; a hundred members of the audience sat on the stage, the rest occupied the auditorium and its galleries.

In this production, Okhlopkov uses attendants in blue masks and dominoes—figures from the pages of Jacques Callot —to serve as property men in the Chinese manner. They move about the stage in full light, distributing props: a telephone, for example, which one of them holds while a character makes a call; then, when the call is completed, takes off the stage. When a table is needed, two others bring on a rectangular piece of green baize; squatting on the floor, they hold it taut while characters gather around it in conference. By such means, Okhlopkov reminds the audience that no matter how realistic a picture of life in a labor camp this may be, it is still only a theatrical presentation and is to be accepted as such.

Perhaps one reason the revival of *Aristocrats* seems less iconoclastic to the Westerner than it originally did is that in the intervening twenty-five years we have become acquainted with the theatrical style of Bertolt Brecht. Whether the Berliner Ensemble owes a debt to Okhlopkov or whether the latter was influenced by the Germans, I am not sure; but there is a close affinity between the two in their style of staging. It is probably no coincidence that Okhlopkov's theatre presented Moscow theatregoers with their first view of Brecht in a Russian production of *Mother Courage* in the autumn of 1960. Even as Meierhold had done before them, both Okhlopkov and Brecht have dismissed the "fourth wall" from their theatres (that imaginary barrier established along the footlights to enable an actor to feel that his world is bounded by the stage). Both demand direct communication between performer and spectator to the extent that the material of the author will permit. Yet, whereas Brecht's theatre seeks to banish emotion, Okhlopkov's exploits it. And herein the latter differs also from Meierhold. In comparing Meierhold's and Okhlopkov's use of direct address, I observed in 1935 that the former ". . . spoke with a subtlety of speech

and a use of symbol which estranged [the audience], perhaps
ever so slightly and it may be subconsciously. Still he talked
at them rather than *with* them, and in doing so he lost his
chance to win them. Okhlopkov's actors seem to talk *with*
their hearers." Okhlopkov feels that in the more direct communion which his physical form of production encourages,
there can be a deepening of emotional impact rather than a
dilution. The action that surges around and through the
audience has as its purpose that audience's complete involvement.

There is certainly no great subtlety at the Mayakovski
Theatre today, and there is no steely sharpness such as one
remembers in Meierhold's Theatre. There is not the wit
either. Instead, there is a broadness, a boldness, and a boister-
ousness (when humor is called for) that makes Okhlopkov
seem vulgar alongside the remembered image of Meierhold.
But this, I suspect, is the former's salvation. He is not likely
to be accused of "estheticism," as was his master, for he has
kept himself basically unsophisticated. He has kept in touch
with the people—including the political powers, who in many
lands beside Russia are not noted for the sensitivity of their
artistic appreciation.

Okhlopkov is a slightly anomalous figure. Reuben Simonov,
Managing Director of the Vakhtangov Theatre, put his finger
on it when he remarked, in an article in the Soviet journal
Teatr, that he was "trying hard to understand Okhlopkov's
position. If Okhlopkov were developing the views of his
teacher, Meierhold, such a policy would be clear to me. If,
on the contrary, he had completely changed and gone over
to Stanislavski or Vakhtangov, I might understand that, too.
But when I see him meditating on realism *and* conventions,
that means that he hesitates between the two." Okhlopkov
replied subsequently in the same journal that he had created

no school. "I am only one of those who try to get results from
a 'crossing' of two theatrical cultures—Stanislavski's and
Meierhold's," he wrote. And he added, quite properly, that
Simonov's master, Vakhtangov, was the first to do just that.

The series of articles contributed to *Teatr* by many of the
leading Soviet stage directors, over a period of some months
at the end of 1959 and well into 1960, threw considerable
light not only on their authors but also on the common problem with which they were all wrestling—how to rediscover
individual styles and still not deny the socialist realism which
remains the official line. Okhlopkov led off the series with a
piece entitled "On the Conventional," in which he seemed
to be saying that, since realism is itself actually only an
artistic convention, so those traditional styles referred to as
"conventional" should be just as acceptable as realism. "The
new world is too new and grandiose, too romantic and
poetic to be shown within the frame of the traditional
everyday-life play and old theatrical technique," he wrote.
"Painting, music, sculpture—these arts have very definite
conventions that are part of their very nature, that everyone
is used to; no one thinks these conventions subversive toward
realism. But it is different for the theatre. There, in the
struggle against formalism, we often 'threw out the baby
along with the bathwater.'" The echoes of Meierhold ring
through the whole article, but never sound louder than at
this moment of self-criticism, when Okhlopkov quotes a
homely adage which Meierhold had used in his valedictory.

Okhlopkov was inveighing against the confinement of
realism when he went on to say, "A storm at sea, a fire on the
steppes, a popular fete—the stage has no ways to show all
these, while the motion pictures can do them easily. We try
to avoid many difficulties (like storms, etc.), because to show
storms and ships naturally is not to be thought of; and so we
limit ourselves to the old pavilion or garden. . . . Most con-

temporary plays, it is true, have little of the fantastic. But perhaps the reason there are so few plays in which the author gives free rein to his imagination is because he knows they could not be performed. And how indeed can we do so with naturalistic heaviness and illusionistic falsification? The theatre has lost the secret. Authors are used to the idea that it is unable to rise above the most simple elements of day-to-day life."

Then Okhlopkov issued his challenge. "I defy all *régisseurs* and designers to do anything about it without using the popular traditions of theatrical convention. There is nothing that the theatre cannot show by its own peculiar means. But it must search for novelties." In these words the descendant of Meierhold restates his master's thesis and makes his contribution toward strengthening the "Meierhold tradition." Never in his exposition does he clearly define what he means by "popular traditions of theatrical convention." But he has shown us in his theatre. There, he establishes himself as opposing Stanislavski's dictum of "banish the theatre from the theatre." He says, in effect, "We do not go to the theatre to forget we are in a theatre. We go to it because it takes us away from life. It is like going to the circus. There we accept the convention of the clown's white cheeks, his huge red mouth, and his enormous flapping shoes. We are not fooled into thinking this 'real.' He is a clown and that is enough for us."

The tightrope Okhlopkov must walk as he proceeds on his chosen path is, nevertheless, extremely tricky. Even as he proclaims for the "theatre theatrical," he says that he seeks today to "study the labyrinth of the inner man more profoundly" than he sought to do twenty-five years ago. We were sitting in his office in what used to be the Theatre of the Revolution (now the Mayakovski). That theatre, incidentally, was

founded by Meierhold as an experimental laboratory—Mayakovski's today, Meierhold's yesterday. As we talked, Okhlopkov continued to paraphrase his recent article. "At the end
of their lives, Stanislavski and Meierhold did not find themselves very far apart. Actually, they were tunneling toward
each other. For example, Meierhold never allowed actors to
sit around a table reading a play in early rehearsals. In his
last days, neither did Stanislavski."

He asked rhetorically, "What is the best form to be chosen
for the expression of the performed ideas of a contemporary
play?" Then he replied to his own question, "There are many
such forms, and they will all do—on one condition only: that
they be so vivid as to make the spectator believe in the reality
of what he sees. The conventional in the theatre must have
as its aim not the theatricalization or 're-theatricalization' of
the stage, as George Fuchs terms it, but life truth and the expression of high ideas. Let there be different styles in the
theatres, including those that try to reproduce as many life-
like details as possible, though I personally think that in this
case the spectator loses great opportunities to use his creative
imagination. But let us have no narrow circle, in which the
so-called orthodox critics would like to shut up all art. I vote
for confidence in the different creative trends in the art of
socialist realism. One and the same high aim may be reached
by different paths." Okhlopkov continued by contrasting
"false conventions, cardboard conventions inherited from
pseudo-classicism, and harmful conventions of the esthetes"
with what he called "a different kind of convention—that of
the popular theatre."

The epic and the grandiose have always appealed to
Okhlopkov. His first work was the staging, at the age of
twenty-one, of a mass drama in a public square in Irkutsk in
Siberia. He still cherishes photographs of that work. His
recent staging of the operatic version of Gorki's *Mother* for

the Bolshoi has a magnificent, epic sweep to it. His production of *An Irkutsk Story* has turned that tale of simple
workers into a sort of twentieth-century epic, in which the
rumbling undertone of drums, the swelling choral singing,
and a slowly revolving stage combine to make the heart beat
faster and the tears flow more readily. In January, 1961, he
was scheduled to complete work on a production of Euripides'
Medea for presentation in Moscow's Chaikovski Hall. There
would be a chorus of about forty women, a choir of nearly
one hundred voices, together with the accompaniment of
a full symphony orchestra.* This is a scale in which he feels
at home. His long-cherished desire is to stage *War and Peace*
as a drama. This would allow him to alternate intimate scenes
with panoramic spectacle. I dare say he will do it someday.

Okhlopkov delights in showing visitors to his present
frankly inadequate playhouse the model of the theatre of the
future toward which he looks. His future theatre will be
circular, with a domed roof that can slide back to reveal the
night sky. Its flexibility will be such that it can resemble a
Renaissance theatre derived from Roman design, with a stage
at one end and a semicircular amphitheatre enclosing an
orchestra; by rearrangement, its tiers of three thousand seats
can be swung around to enclose a complete arena; then the
seats can be rearranged again so that action can surround the
spectators. This would be a place for *War and Peace!* It is a
plan of which Meierhold would have approved.

It is in the field of satire that Okhlopkov's contribution to
the maintenance of a Meierhold tradition falls short. Meier-

---

* This production finally opened, almost a year behind schedule, and
promptly became the most talked-of theatrical event of Moscow's 1961–1962
season. When witnessing this "epic tragedy of the human spirit rebeling
against insupportable injustice," Harrison E. Salisbury reported to the New
York *Times* that some of the beholders felt "that there, but for a whim of
destiny, they might have stood during the terror of the time of Stalin."

hold was a master satirist. His production of Gogol's *The Inspector-General,* probably the greatest satiric work for the stage in all Russian literature, was his undisputed masterpiece, doubtless because the twentieth-century director found in Gogol a genius to complement his own perfectly. It was, in fact, this strong vein of irony and satire which contributed to Meierhold's downfall. The weapon of laughter is invaluable in destruction; it is useless, even dangerous when the day of destruction ends and is supplanted by a period of affirmation and construction. The Stalinists found nothing to laugh at in their march toward socialism. So Meierhold's weapon was of no use to them, and he could find no compatibility in their earnest outlook.

But the Russian temperament possesses a strong streak of the ironic; the Russian loves to laugh. Laughter could not be denied him forever. Therefore, when the Twentieth Party Congress signaled the beginning of a relaxation from Stalinist tensions, satire was one of the first things to be resuscitated on the stage. This was not, however, accomplished by Okhlopkov. Instead, one must turn to another theatre, the Theatre of Satire, for nowhere was the relaxation from Stalinist tensions more quickly or effectively accomplished than here.

What I have to say of the Theatre of Satire is largely second-hand, for aside from performances I witnessed there, I had no direct contact with it. I would like to note the reason for this omission. The Artistic Director of this theatre, Valentin Pluchek, was a man I had not known in the 1930's, so, shortly after my arrival in Moscow, I requested the Ministry of Culture to arrange a meeting. Despite frequent reminders, no appointment was forthcoming. Subsequently, I repeated my request more than once to the Society for Friendship and Cultural Relations with Foreign Countries. Again my request was ignored. It was obvious that the

Russian authorities did not want me to establish a connection with the Theatre of Satire. This was underscored by the fact that when I submitted a list of productions in various Moscow theatres (the Theatre of Satire among them) of which I would like photographs, none was forthcoming from that company. No explanation was ever made.

However, in tracing the Meierhold tradition, the Theatre of Satire cannot be ignored. It is, in fact, along with the Sovremennik, the Mayakovski, and the Vakhtangov, one of the four most interesting theatres in Moscow today. Furthermore, it strikes me as being the one theatre in Moscow that is in considerably better artistic shape than it was twenty-five years ago. Perhaps it is a little *too* interesting. Satire poses a delicate problem in all authoritarian states, and its place in such a state is bound to be insecure. Wherever criticism is controlled, the question arises: How can satire be countenanced? The answer is that criticism may have a voice—so long as the ruling authority considers it to be valid and justified. One of Moscow's leading drama critics solemnly explained to me, "No one thinks everything here is perfect. All sorts of things need improving, from the service in restaurants to individual human foibles. To make fun of these things in the theatre is as effective in getting them changed and improved as to write censorious editorials in the papers. Satire is therefore highly regarded—that is, of course, when it is helpful." In other words, as long as he does not make fun of the wrong people or the wrong things, the door is wide open to the satirist.

Okhlopkov's theatre is called the Theatre of Mayakovski. Over his desk hangs a line-drawing portrait of Mayakovski, and there is a bust of Mayakovski in the theatre's foyer. Yet, in the autumn of 1960, no play by Mayakovski was in the repertoire of the company that bears his name. Instead, one

had to go to the Theatre of Satire to see the two examples of
his works then visible in Moscow, *The Bedbug* and *The
Bathhouse*.

Vladimir Mayakovski, primarily a poet, secondarily a dramatist, was one of the outstanding men of letters of his generation.
Meierhold staged his work with delight. Mayakovski's *Mystery Bouffe* was one of the great director's early productions
after the Revolution. The young poet's boundless energy, his
exaggerated theatricality, his trenchant verse, his sharp wit
were completely in tune with Meierhold's own temperament.
The great *régisseur* loved to have the poet around. "I have
been staging plays for many years," Meierhold once wrote,
"but I never allowed myself the luxury of letting a dramatist
work with me directing a play. Yet not only did I permit
Mayakovski to work with me; I found I could not work without him."

It may seem odd that I made no mention of Mayakovski's
name or his work in the pages of *Moscow Rehearsals*. The
reason for this omission is that, during the years immediately
following his suicide in 1930, Mayakovski's theatrical works
were unproduced. They were not banned, as far as I know;
they simply did not appeal to audiences, and so went off the
boards. The public was apparently made uncomfortable by
Mayakovskian exaggerations and pyrotechnics. Perhaps it
sensed disillusionment behind the running fire of "gags" and
did not wish nor dare to come to grips with it. In any case,
all has now changed in the 1950's and 1960's. Mayakovski's
poetry has been republished, his plays have been revived on
the stage, and the public today adores this man of the early
Revolution. It is easy to see why: His theatre is hilarious;
it is also the theatre of a poet.

Actors performing Mayakovski's works, Victor Komissarzhevski quite correctly observes, "must be masters of the
word, must use the word sharpened to the point of genuine

poetry. His is a theatre of inordinate energy. Each character
is literally obsessed with his own ideas and passions. This is
the source of all its exaggerations, of the hyperbolic effect of
its images. It is a spectacular theatre, a theatre that presents
the truth of life in festive and symbolic form." Mayakovski,
in point of fact, called *The Bathhouse* a "drama with circus
and fireworks" and termed *The Bedbug* an "extravaganza."
"It washes—simply wipes out—the bureaucrats," he claimed.
As in *The Bedbug, The Bathhouse* accomplishes its ends by
transferring the action to the future by means, in this instance, of a time machine. The presentation of these Mayakovski plays is the crowning achievement of the Theatre of
Satire.

But the company also has other fare to offer. From the
satiric novels of Ilya Ilf and Eugene Petrov come two deli-
ciously amusing adaptations: *Twelve Chairs* and its sequel,
The Little Golden Calf. Both of these make fun of the petit-
bourgeois remnants that hung on after the Revolution. As in
The Bedbug, the plays are set in the period of the New
Economic Policy of the early twenties. The story of *Twelve
Chairs,* for example, concerns an ex-nobleman, Vorobyaninov,
who learns from his mother-in-law on her deathbed that the
family jewels have been secreted in one of the family's dining-
room chairs. Unfortunately, the set of twelve chairs has been
broken up and disposed of in a dozen directions. Vorobyaninov sets out to discover the chair that contains the cache of
diamonds. He is joined in his search by Ostap Bender, a
"smooth operator" who is really a resourceful crook; and
together the treasure hunters sally forth, meeting along their
journey a wild assortment of hypocrites, fools, and knaves.

It would seem that all this is quite recognizable and,
indeed, rather endearing to today's Soviet citizens, judging
from their reception of it. Perhaps this is because more than
the petit bourgeoisie is under inspection. Maurice Friedberg

has put his finger on the enduring popularity of these plays in writing in an introduction to *Twelve Chairs* that "Ostap Bender is a Soviet crook, born of Soviet conditions and quite willing to coexist with the Soviet system to which he has no ideological or even economic objections. . . . He also knows that the Soviet Man is not very different from the Capitalist Man—that he is just as greedy, lazy, snobbish, cowardly, and gullible—and [he] uses these weaknesses to his [own] advantage." If this is not risky subject matter, then the regime is feeling more secure than most Americans think. But, looking at it strictly from an artistic point of view, which is my principal concern, it should be noted that, as in the Mayakovski productions in this theatre, there are Meierholdian touches to be found in the production of *Twelve Chairs:* exaggerated make-ups and postures, bright nonliteral scenery. It is, in short, all "theatre theatrical."

In the autumn of 1960, the Theatre of Satire presented a production of Noel Coward's *Nude with Violin.* It is the only production of Coward in the Soviet Union of which I have ever heard, and *Izvestia's* review of the first performance provides some interesting clues to the reaction of the Communist world on being exposed to the darling of Belgravia. Said *Izvestia:*

This play is a frank paradox, and this quality is stressed in each episode. First we see the cupidity of the respectable relatives who are after the dead painter's inheritance. Then we learn that the celebrity was nothing but a fake. All his pictures were done by other people, who appear before the surprised family. More than that we see grotesque monsters—religious fanatics, cynical children, prostitutes, pimps, swindlers. Sebastian played a cruel trick upon the so-called "connoisseurs," but he did it to prove that true art has nothing to do with the miserable daubs of his dissolute friends. He planned a colossal exposure, but it all turns into a colossal farce. Truth did not come out; his accomplice's silence was bought with his own money. All remains the same, and so it ends.

We see that the play is unusual. The author is more interested in his paradoxes and the different plot developments than in real characters and circumstances. Abstract art is meaningless, says he, and he proves it by paradoxical means; and he is successful because what he laughs at has been exposed long. . . .

The performance is less sarcastic and funny than the play.

The world moves on when Mr. Coward has made his debut in Moscow!

Today, the Theatre of Satire is approximately thirty years old. In its early seasons it presented topical revues that carried such titillating titles as *You Aren't a Hooligan, Are You, Citizen?* and *Moscow From the Viewpoint Of.* By 1934, however, unfortunately it had stopped presenting topical revues; and, in 1935, I was treated instead to a domestic comedy called *Somebody Else's Baby,* which was neither satiric nor very funny. It was, however, a smash hit which tided the theatre over (along with some classical comedies) until the war. Then, during the ensuing period, comedy dwindled, as the Soviets devoted their stage to the depiction of World War II. There followed years of empty comedies, for this theatre, like all the others, suffered from the leveling process that destroyed initiative. Then, with the thaw of 1956 and the rediscovery of Mayakovski plus the appearance of Pluchek as the principal *régisseur,* the Theatre of Satire experienced a regeneration.

I wish I felt that the Theatre of Satire's future is secure. Certainly, the local citizens love it. The faces one encounters there are young and intelligent. But I ask myself why I was prevented from hearing its story at first hand. After one has spent a few months in the U.S.S.R., one grows suspicious about such things.

7

The Vakhtangov

Tradition

Of all the theatres in Moscow today, the soundest strikes me
as being the Vakhtangov. It is not the most startling;
Okhlopkov's, in the tradition of Meierhold, is that. It is not
the most youthfully dynamic; the Sovremennik, in the tradition of Stanislavski, is that. It is not the most famous; the
Moscow Art Theatre and the Maly—abroad and at home,
respectively—are that. But the Vakhtangov Theatre has a
vigor, a strength, and a creativity which express themselves
in a multiplicity of ways, and which are nevertheless combined with a unity of approach that gives this theatre authority without allowing it to become academic. Eugene
Vakhtangov died almost forty years ago, but the theatre that
bears his name today is as clear about his aims as though he
had died only yesterday. Furthermore, his followers are as
committed to those aims as they were in 1921 or in 1935.

Vakhtangov grew up in the Moscow Art Theatre (even as
Meierhold had some twenty years earlier) as one of Stani-

slavski's aptest pupils. The Revolution, breaking out just as he was reaching his artistic maturity, affected his thinking and his feeling more profoundly than it did his elders at the MXAT. Thus, it was almost inevitable that he should break away to begin his own personal quest for expression in art, an expression which would be based on a Marxist interpretation.

Vakhtangov's break was not as profound as that of Meierhold. He believed, with Stanislavski, that the art of the theatre must spring from life and be grounded in its truth. He accepted the Stanislavski system, one of whose aims, as stated by its creator, "was to give practical and conscious methods for the awakening of superconscious creativeness." But it was Vakhtangov's belief that his followers should practice this method only *up to a point:* They were to stop short of "becoming" the character they were enacting. They were, in fact, to shed subjectivity and assume an objective attitude; they were not to "reproduce" life on the stage, but were to remain always slightly outside it so that they could make their own comment on it. When Vakhtangov said, "Look at life and make that your guide in creation," he sounded like Stanislavski, but actually he meant more than is at first suggested. He really meant, "Look at life in its entire social context. Recreate in your acting not only the physical image of a man, his emotions, his thoughts, what you can capture of his spirit; recreate also the image of that man in the world of which he is a part." This was Vakhtangov's first commandment.

His second commandment rose out of his first: The actor must not only develop a distinct image in his creative imagination, but he must also take a conscious position in relation to it. It is not enough to play Hamlet with truth, not enough to relate him to his world. The actor must develop a passionate attitude toward Hamlet. Either he must fall in love with him or he must despise him. He must never be neutral in feeling. Only by following this admonition can the actor arrive at that basic position from which he can make his comment and persuade his public that it is valid.

Today, Vakhtangov's heirs pledge their continuing allegiance to another principle which was originally enunciated by their leader. This third commandment is: "If an artist wants to create after the Revolution, he must create together with the people—not for their sake, not out of them, but together with them." This statement I presume to have more than one application. It demands a sense of comradeship between the artist and his public within the playhouse, as in the word "communion" which Okhlopkov uses. Translated into theatrical terms, this means demanding that the actor take the audience into his confidence, breaking the psychological barrier of the fourth-wall convention of realism. The actor must play in such a way that, if it is not actually to his audience, the audience still knows that he is aware of their presence and that he is involved with them in this evening's experience. Beyond this, the dictum means a general sense of "togetherness" with the world outside the theatre, without which the artist so easily tends to become self-absorbed and isolated.

This sense of comradeship, Vakhtangov felt, must, like charity, begin at home. Theatrical production is a collective enterprise wherever in the world it takes place. The way to achieve the finest results is by emphasizing this collectiveness rather than, as Meierhold did and as Okhlopkov is rather apt to do, by minimizing it. Vakhtangov felt that the "whole collective of the theatre must participate in the plot of the *régisseur* and of the dramatist. . . . The spirit of the new Russia must have its expression in the theatre collective where all are to share in a common creative experience."

In theory, all this is admirable, and I believe that no enduringly great theatre can exist unless all members of it are made to feel a community of aim and a mutual dependence. In practice, however, I have seldom seen it work without strong leadership. Therefore, paradoxical as it may seem, if the leader is imbued with this sense of "one for all and all for one," the entire group can rise beyond the capacities of its leader, no matter how talented that one man may be. In this regard, Vakhtangov stood in sharp contrast to Meierhold. Since Meierhold never believed this precept and since he never took his artists into his confidence, his theatre never became any greater than he himself was. Vakhtangov's did, and it remains so.

Morris Carnovsky, the distinguished American actor, put his finger on the well-spring of Vakhtangov's greatness when he said, "One of the greatest experiences that I think I've had in the theatre was the Habimah* *Dybbuk* years ago. . . . Its director had long ago passed away, Vakhtangov of the Russian theatre. . . . For a spell of creation, really like the creation of the world, nothing has paralleled what I felt with that *Dybbuk*. . . . What was this traceable to? I think it was traceable to love . . . I think Vakhtangov loved the material, I think he loved his actors, I think his actors loved him; I think that together they made what is to me the classic experience of the theatre."

Vakhtangov laid down two further precepts. The first of these was a demand for "maximum sharpness and definite form." There is a brightness in every production of the Vakhtangov Theatre which results, I believe, from the appli-

---

* Prior to founding the theatre that now bears his name, Vakhtangov had directed a Hebrew company in Moscow called the Habimah (or Habima), which came to New York in 1926 during a world tour and settled subsequently in Palestine.

cation of this principle. The words "maximum sharpness" and "definite form" refer to external effect, an element highly valued on the Vakhtangov stage. It is an element related in turn to a basic attitude toward the theatre which can best be summed up in the word "enjoyment." Reuben Simonov, Artistic Director of the Vakhtangov, recently remarked that the theatre "deprived of the elements of play . . . loses the festive character that is in its very nature." The Vakhtangov likes to play. If, in the drab days between 1937 and 1957, this theatre lost its sense of fete, I am glad I was not in Moscow to witness it. Whatever it may then have undergone, however, it is now moving back toward that bright sharpness of form, that jocund air to which Vakhtangov himself gave perfect expression in his unforgettable *Princess Turandot,* which was performed more than a thousand times. In that production, the actors indulged in a series of carnival improvisations. Arriving on stage in evening dress, they fashioned costumes out of whatever props they could lay their hands on. Towels wrapped around their heads became turbans, scarves tied to chins became beards, they donned commedia dell'arte masks and proceeded to give a performance of Carlo Gozzi's fairy tale of an Eastern land that blended sophisticated theatricality with the naïve "let's make believe" playing of children.

Vakhtangov's final precept was that each play should dictate its own style of performance. He sought constantly to prevent his theatre from establishing one set approach to every work of art. He deplored the practice of the MXAT which produced every play from Shakespeare to Chekhov in the style of psychological realism; and of Meierhold, who denied psychological motivations altogether, demanding that every play be mounted in terms of his favorite theory of "biomechanics." Each play is a unique creation, argued

Alexandra Yablochkina, now in her nineties, personifies the Maly Theatre's tradition of realism. Here, she appears as Miss Crawley in *Vanity Fair*.

A merry-go-round swings the principal characters of *Vanity Fair* onto the stage of the Maly in a rare moment of tradition-shattering theatricality.

The Moscow Art Theatre's production of *The Cherry Orchard* is still performed in the realistic tradition of Stanislavski. Alla Tarasova *(seated at left center)* appears as Madame Ranvevskaya.

The Moscow Art Theatre's revival of *The Sea Gull* differs from earlier Chekhovian productions in that it combines stylistic and realistic elements in an otherwise traditional garden setting.

At twenty-three, Edward Martsevich, the Hamlet of the Mayakovski Theatre, is Moscow's youngest leading man.

The old Meierholdian tradition of frank theatricality is evident in the Mayakovski Theatre's production of Shakespeare's *Hamlet*. In this scene, the popular uprising against King Claudius at the time of Laertes' home-

Martsevich's youthful Hamlet lacks intellectual depth, but has made the actor the idol of Moscow's bobby-soxers.

coming *(left)*, which is usually limited to offstage "alarums," is fully exploited on stage. *(Above)* **Elsinore Castle is** dramatically set as a beehive of leaden cells.

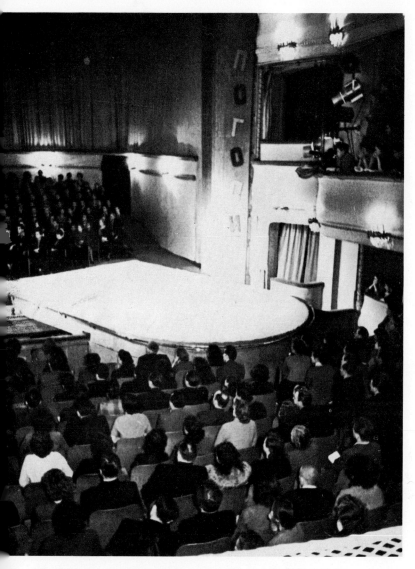

The Mayakovski Theatre's revival of Nikolai Pogodin's *Aristocrats* uses the two stages of the modified theatre-in-the-round, which Nikolai Okhlopkov employed in his original 1935 production.

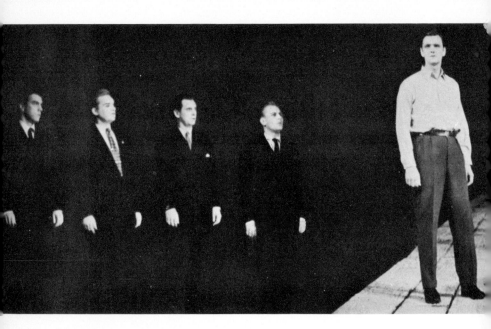

In the Vakhtangov Theatre's production of *An Irkutsk Story,* a happy
Soviet father brings his wife and newborn twins home from the hospital.

The current hit play of Moscow, *An Irkutsk Story*, by Alexei Arbuzov, is a lyrical interpretation of life and love on a hydroelectric project.

Facing Page

Yuri Yakovlev, one of three great young
artists of the Vakhtangov Theatre,
shows versatility as the optimistic Rodik
(left) of *An Irkutsk Story* and as the brooding
Prince Myshkin *(right)* of *The Idiot.*

Facing Page

Julia Borisova of the Vakhtangov portrays
the modern and tempestuous Valya *(left)*
of Arbuzov's *An Irkutsk Story* and
(right) the elegant Nastasya Filippovna of
Dostoyevski's *The Idiot.*

Facing Page

Mikhail Ulyanov appears at the Vakhtangov
as the model, well-adjusted hydroelectric
project worker, Sergei *(left)* of *An Irkutsk
Story* and as the anguished Rogozhin
(right) of *The Idiot.*

In the famous banquet scene from Maxim Gorki's *Foma Gordeyev*, old "capitalists" sing "God Save the Tsar." The scene is done in the Vakhtangov Theatre's traditional style of caricature.

The same satirical elements are more broadly exaggerated by
Designer G. B. Shchukin in his sketch of the banquet scene.

The fairy tale, *Aladdin*, staged for children by Sergei Obraztsov at the great Central Puppet Theatre, relies on wit, inventiveness, and superb caricature.

The problem play, *My Friend Kolka*, staged for teen-agers by Anatoly Efros at the Central Children's Theatre, explores nonconformity among Soviet youth.

The ideal Soviet theatre, as envisioned by Nikolai Okhlopkov of the Mayakovski Theatre, would be a ribbed, futuristic structure whose dome could be opened to the sky and whose movable stage and three thousand seats could be rearranged to create innumerable performer-spectator relationships.

Vakhtangov; every playwright is a being alone. What may work stylistically for Gorki will not do for Gozzi. In Broadway parlance, what Vakhtangov was demanding was that his theatre should never allow itself to become "type cast."

If such a precept had been his sole aim, it could have quickly resulted in a sort of "all-things-to-all-men" eclecticism that would eventually have robbed the Vakhtangov Theatre of its individuality. But this was not so. It was by no means Vakhtangov's one concern, for combined with it were all those other elements that made up his search for a positive creative line. As a result, this very flexibility is today one of the Vakhtangov's most distinctive characteristics.

During World War II a bomb fell in Arbat Street and destroyed the Vakhtangov Theatre's building. Today, on the same site, stands a new playhouse. It has some of the same functional air that I well recall characterized its predecessor: flatly painted, sand-colored walls; an almost-matching curtain; little ornamentation. It is the right size—approximately one thousand seats—for the well-being of its audience. (Unfortunately, the auditorium is for some reason situated one flight above the street level, as are the auditoriums of the MXAT and the Theatre of Satire, its staircases thereby creating unnecessary bottlenecks when the play is over, though these are no worse than London's, where the stalls are often one flight below street level.) It has huge foyers, whose walls are lined with portraits of the company and with photographs of productions, and it has a large buffet. For the comfort of the artists, there are equally spacious accommodations backstage. The Artistic Director is well provided for, too; he has a handsome office with ultramarine walls and Empire furniture and a reception room adjoining his stage-left box.

In the first eight weeks of the 1960–1961 season, the

repertoire of this theatre showed an almost even balance
between contemporary and classical works. Out of the past
were Chekhov's *Piece Without a Name* (also called *Platonov*
and performed in New York in 1960 as *A Country Incident*),
Dostoyevski's *The Idiot,* Alexander Fredro's *The Ladies and
the Hussars,* Gorki's *Foma Gordeyev,* Hauptmann's *Before
Sundown,* Mamin-Sebriak's *In the Golden Depths,* Pushkin's
*Three Short Tragedies—The Miserly Knight, Mozart and
Salieri,* and *The Stone Guest*—and Shakespeare's *Hamlet*
(which was given a single performance during those two
months). From modern times came two plays by Arbuzov,
An Irkutsk Story and *The Twelfth Hour; Alone* by Aleshin;
The Cook by Sofronov; *The Sixth Floor* by the Frenchman,
Alfred Gehri; and *Filumena Marturano* by the Italian,
Eduardo de Filippo (the latter two being the only contempo-
rary foreign works).

It would not be possible for me to say that each of these
plays was performed in a different style, since I did not see all
fourteen productions. But by contrasting three of them, I
can perhaps illustrate Vakhtangov's dictum that "each play
must have its own style." Let us take *The Idiot, The Ladies
and the Hussars,* and *An Irkutsk Story.*

The tone of Arbuzov's play is set by Julia Borisova, who
plays the girl Valya, around whom the action centers. It is for
this actress, I am told, that the play was written; and insofar
as it is a realistic drama of contemporary life, the Vakhtangov
production infuses it with psychological truth. But during the
early part of the play, Borisova's coarse blonde wig, her
raucous voice, and her slightly undulating hips convey both
the image of the kind of girl Valya is and also, in a subtle
way, the actress' own opinion of such a girl. As Valya grows
in stature, Borisova's sympathy for her increases. Her portrayal softens, and, at the end, it opens into fresh new vigor
as the performer seems to applaud the character she is enact-

ing. This is how Vakhtangov's theory of the artist's relation
to his role translates itself in specific terms.

Insofar as *An Irkutsk Story* is more than a realistic play—
through the use Arbuzov makes, for instance, of a chorus to
give the drama a retrospective tone (almost as Tennessee
Williams does through a narrator in *The Glass Menagerie*)
and perhaps also to expand its social implications—Yevgeny
Simonov, its director, has superimposed special stylistic effects. Projected backgrounds impressionistically suggest the
limitless wastes of Siberia, in the heart of which man wrestles
with nature. Musical themes are hauntingly reiterated. There
is a curious blend of the sympathetic and the impersonal in
the four men who compose the chorus. All these contributions make the performance eminently theatrical at the same
time that it is moving in its human believability.

Now, take the two classics and contrast their productions
with that of *An Irkutsk Story*. When the curtain rises on *The
Idiot,* the spectator is projected back into nineteenth-century
Russian theatre. The exteriors are scrupulously literal in
their rendering of every rock and rill. Realistic birch foliage
billows overhead, supported by scrim net. In the interiors
the samovars steam and the cold northern sunlight streams
through long, curtained windows. The sounds of the railway
car on which Prince Myshkin travels, indeed almost the
smells of his jolting journey, are faithfully reproduced. All
the characters are psychologically recreated with the same
diligent care. In the ballroom each guest is a carefully drawn
portrait in miniature.

"This performance seems to me more like the Art
Theatre's than the Vakhtangov's," I said to Simonov as I bade
him good night at its conclusion.

"Precisely," he replied. "That is the way Dostoyevski must
be played. Don't forget, each playwright has his own style
and our job is to find what is right for him. We cannot play

The Idiot as we would play *An Irkutsk Story*. For Dostoyevski, the Stanislavski approach is the correct one. Why should
we treat it differently and be incorrect?"

What is right for Dostoyevski would certainly not be right
for the nineteenth-century Polish farceur, Fredro, either. The
Vakhtangov's presentation of *The Ladies and the Hussars,* a
minor work in the history of world literature, is all fun and
festivity, full of the brightness and sharpness that come
straight down in the Vakhtangov tradition from *Princess
Turandot.* The story is inconsequential, possibly not as
complicated as *An Italian Straw Hat* of Eugène Labiche, but
of much the same genre. Briefly, it is the tale of how three
sisters plan the marriage of Sophia, the daughter of one of
them, to a young hussar, and of how the girl deceives the
middle-aged major who also seeks her favors. All ends happily, and the public loves it.

Communion with the audience is complete. Ladies in hoop
skirts, spit curls, and parasols, followed by their escorting
dandies, who carry the ladies' bird cages and portmanteaus,
are incessantly running up and down the aisles, shouting at
the characters on the stage, clambering over the footlights—
the house lights being turned on fully the while. There are
constant asides to the audience, spoken by characters leaning
against the proscenium arch or coming down stage center.
There is a small orchestra dressed in the costumes of the
period that is seated eight feet off the ground on one side of
the stage; its conductor is constantly dragged into the action.
Songs and dances are performed with ingenuous good humor
whenever the story becomes a bit labored. It is hard to believe
that this is the same company that the night before performed
that dark and complex tragedy, *The Idiot.*

But it would not be fair to leave you with this image of a
bit of confection, all stuff and no substance. To be sure, one
does not ask substance of a farce; but there was in the playing

of Yuri Yakovlev, as the stout and aging major, a richness
that made the butt of the play's joke more than a mere figure
of fun. This very able young actor of thirty gave stature to
the whole production, even as a fine actor playing M. Jourdain can remind us of the true humanity that underlies
Molière's farce, *Le Bourgeois Gentilhomme*. Working with
no more material than the other actors (or so I assume, since
I have not read the play in the original Polish), Yakovlev
superimposes over the irony and the delicately exaggerated
caricature that the entire cast employs a warmhearted, honest
sincerity that is completely disarming. I suppose it is the
result of Vakhtangov's commandment concerning the actor's
role: Yakovlev, the actor, seems to have fallen in love with
the character of the major, and he conveys this to us. He
never goes to the extremes of, for instance, a Bert Lahr; but
he does manage to make us simultaneously laugh at him and
love him, even as Lahr can do. Yet this young Russian's
talent is more remarkable than is Lahr's, for the latter's
range is limited; whereas Yakovlev is equally persuasive as
the brooding and mad Prince Myshkin in the film version of
The Idiot, a role that I would hate, with all due respect, to
see Mr. Lahr undertake.

In *The Ladies and the Hussars*, Yakovlev admirably illus-
trates the real virtuosity which a leading actor at the Vakhtangov must possess, if he is to fulfill completely the injunction of his master to perform each play in the style that it
demands. The importance of such virtuosity is stressed by
Reuben Simonov: "The actor of today must possess perfect
inner technique, must develop all 'his means and abilities,' as
Vakhtangov phrased it, if he is to impersonate perfectly any
form demanded of him by us, his *régisseurs*." One can assume
that Simonov, as the Artistic Director of the Vakhtangov, was
speaking for that collective in the controversy among directors which raged last year in *Teatr*, when he went on to take

the following position: "The main force in the theatre is [not the *régisseur,* not the dramatist. It is] the actor. The spectator sees people first; their thoughts and feelings are conveyed to him by the actor. The theatre's level is defined by the quality of the actor, his technique, his ability to interpret the high ideas of the play. I believe that the theatre of the future must be primarily a theatre of great actors." Then, in words that sound as though addressed to those American devotees of "the Method," who have acquired their knowledge of it third-hand, Simonov says, "The notion that it suffices to 'live' one's part and [that] the character will be created of itself is the most harmful of notions. From 'emotion' to the embodiment of that emotion on the stage, the path is long and arduous. Let us think over the words we use every day: performance, act, actor. There is a definite meaning in them. When I go onto the stage, I say, 'I'm going to act'; never do I say, 'I'm going to feel emotions.' Is it not worth-while to reconsider terminology? Had we not better free the words 'performance' and 'acting' from the obnoxious connotations they have acquired, owing to different misinterpretations of the great Stanislavski's theory?"

In this article, Simonov then offers Vakhtangov's alternative to the theatre of emotion. The actor's highest artistic achievement, he claims, lies in the element of "show." A man does not as a rule become an actor because he wants to submerge his own personality in a series of other people's, but because he wants to show himself to others. This instinct toward "showmanship" must, according to Simonov, be cultivated, not suppressed, and indeed it is necessary to achieve exactly this showmanship if one is to bring to a play the true Vakhtangov point of view. Here we have it in a nutshell: the *representation* of life on the stage versus the *presentation,* the showing of life. Simonov, as the leader of Vakhtangov's disciples, restates for today his master's devia-

tion from Stanislavski and reiterates the Vakhtangov tradition: The stage is a place "to show" not "to be."

Ever since the death of its leader, which took place on the
very threshold of its existence, the Vakhtangov company has
had no dominating personality to control it. Yet, in spite of
this lack, it has grown and flourished. Perhaps it is the concept of collective creativeness—which the company inherited
from its founder—that takes the place of the dominating individual. In practice, it works out in the following fashion.
On such major decisions as whether or not to present a particular play, the entire collective votes, and this means several
hundred people, for there are eighty actors alone. If the
Artistic Director decides to disregard an opposing vote and
stage the play anyway, he may assert his authority and do
so. But, as Simonov remarks, he is then very much on the
spot to prove he is right. If he is wrong too many times, the
presumption is that he then forfeits his post, again by vote
of the collective.

Obviously the entire membership of the theatre cannot be
party to every decision, so it elects an Artistic Council of
thirteen members to represent it and to advise the Director
on all but the most important artistic matters such as the
choice of the play or of who should fill the post of Artistic Director. This system was in practice twenty-five
years ago when I first became acquainted with the Vakhtangov, even to the same number of representatives on the
Council. I presume, therefore, that the system works out, or
it would have been altered. Now, as then, the Artistic Council supervises all such matters as the director for a particular
production, the choice of a designer, the solution of major
problems of casting, and the progress of the play to its final
dress rehearsals.

Some of this collective creativeness manifests itself in the rehearsals. In the autumn of 1960, Simonov was rehearsing a play of his own authorship, entitled *Life*. The play had gone into rehearsal in the spring, but there had been a two-month break while the collective had gone on summer holiday, so the first rehearsal I attended, which was the first since spring, was devoted to reëstablishing the action that had been set before the work was interrupted. That morning, at eleven o'clock, the cast assembled in the public buffet of the theatre. The tables and chairs had been pushed back against the walls, except for one small square table at which the director sat by himself. Screens covered with green burlap were so arranged as to outline the acting area of the stage. A staircase needed for the action was provided. Furniture was makeshift, not what would be used in performance. Even in these early rehearsals, however, there were such sound effects as telephone bells and a drum to simulate distant cannonading (for the action takes place in 1919 during the Russian Civil War).

That morning and at every subsequent rehearsal of this play that I attended, I noted a complete absence of tension. Simonov would interrupt from time to time to tell an anecdote; an actor would break off, if something was going uncomfortably, and sit down with the author-director to discuss it in comradely fashion. There was no sense of that pressure which seems always to keep American rehearsals at a kind of fever pitch. There was no such nervous strain as our actors seem constantly to work under—strain induced by fear of the director or of the producer or of fellow actors or by the fear that somehow one may lose his job or displease the boss or the "star." For the director, too, there was no strain resulting from the shortness of time nor from the size of a financial investment which would demand that one come up with a "hit." There was, instead, a remarkably coöperative spirit. The author-director seemed always ready to listen to any actor's suggestion (no matter how minor the actor) on textual alterations, on changes of stage business, or on interpretations of scenes; and the actors seemed to welcome each other's suggestions and criticisms, all openly voiced and discussed.

"I don't think this line gives me enough to get into the scene with," Borisova, who in this play was enacting the mother of two grown boys, said to Simonov. "Can't I add something like this?" and she improvised a bit.

Then Mikhail Ulyanov, who played Borisova's husband, said, "Why should Dima answer the phone? I'm so much nearer. It looks silly for him to cross me to get to it."

"I agree," said Dima, "and while we're on the subject . . ."

The director listened to and encouraged this sort of participation, and, since it is a basic tenet of this theatre that there should be such collective creativeness, everyone spoke up without self-consciousness. Even the fourth-year student from the Shchukin School, who had been brought in to play a minor role, added her voice without diffidence whenever she had an idea relating to her own role or to that of anyone else. At the same time, things never got out of hand. After Simonov had listened to everyone's suggestions and chosen among them, he reëstablished himself as director, and the scene proceeded. The work moved slowly. One day's work might not cover more than a twenty-minute scene, but one could see that scene grow before one's eyes.

Rehearsals lasted only about three hours. At the end of one of them, Simonov escorted me back to his office, where we could sit quietly and talk.

"Don't you think that young girl has talent?" he asked, referring to the student.

I agreed, but I asked why he had chosen her.

"She seems the right age," he replied, "the right type."

"Do you mean to tell me you cast by type? I thought in Moscow this was not done."

"Theoretically, it's not," he said. "Every actor in our theatre should be able to play anything. But, of course, I must in actuality cast to type a good deal of the time. There is no point in having a thirty-year-old woman play an eighteen-year-old, if a good eighteen-year-old girl is available."

Thus was that myth exploded. And it was followed by another.

"When will the play be ready to open?" I asked.

"Probably in six weeks," he replied. "We did a little work on it in the spring, but we're really just starting now."

"Six weeks!" I exclaimed. "Why, it used to take you four or five months!"

"I know," said Simonov. "I've changed my views on rehearsal technique. I no longer believe in a long preparatory reading and discussion period around the table. I understand they have come to the same conclusion even at the MXAT. No, I expect my actors to bring enough depth, understanding, and intelligence to their roles so that a lot of analytical talk is unnecessary. I start off almost at once setting the action. Questions will arise, of course—you've seen that this morning —but they can be coped with as we go along."

I was reminded of Stanislavski's telling me in 1937 that he was coming to the conclusion that physical action held the key to inner truth. I recalled also my recent conversation with Kedrov, in which he confirmed that the Stanislavski system had in effect undergone a one-hundred-and-eighty-degree reversal in the last quarter-century, so that it now starts where it used to end. Now, too, the Vakhtangov Theatre was putting these same ideas into practice.

"A classic, of course, requires more time," Simonov continued. "Probably three or four months. But modern works are not that complicated. You will see! In another month I shall stop rehearsing in the hall and go to the stage. There we shall have the setting, and, of course, many things will be changed. I plan to play a great deal of the action well downstage. Perhaps we'll incorporate the proscenium doors into the plan. It's hard to tell until I actually see it."

I realized that I had seen no notes other than textual alterations to the script. Simonov does not work from a preconceived plot of movement. He allows the movement to evolve and to find its own best way.

"What is important in this production is to establish an intimate atmosphere," Simonov added. "All the action takes place in this family's home. The audience must feel quite close to the people. That's why psychological motivations are so important—so that the public will believe. That's also why I want the action down on the apron."

I wish I could report that the schedule worked out as he anticipated, that six weeks later I was able to attend the première. But, as a matter of fact, two months after this conversation the play had not yet been transferred from the rehearsal hall to the stage. There were, however, reasons for the delay that had nothing to do with artistic theory. One was the same old problem I had encountered in 1935: illness. "The Russian artists are always getting sick!" I exclaimed then, adding that in view of the fact they lead such strenuous lives and that the climate is so rigorous, it is "no wonder illness overtakes them. When it does and an important actor or a number of the lesser ones are sick, rehearsals are simply called off for the time being." So, once again in 1960, excusable absenteeism was playing havoc with the timetable. The other delay was attributable to the fact that Simonov had been commissioned by the Bolshoi Theatre to stage the opera, *Faust*. Unlike in most opera houses outside the Soviet Union, the stage director enters the production picture early and is allowed time to conduct a large number of rehearsals. Few directors can rehearse two productions at once, so

Simonov had to set his own play aside, allowing it to fall
behind schedule in order to fulfill his commitment to the
Bolshoi.

Only in countries like the Soviet Union, where permanent
theatres play in repertory, is it possible for a theatrical management to regard time with such indifference. There is no
problem about productions to fill the theatre, nor about
keeping the contracted artists busy. The Vakhtangov already
had fourteen productions going. The fifteenth would open
when it was ready and not before; deadlines are nonexistent.
There is a long tradition to support this attitude. For more
than half a century, the Moscow Art Theatre, which has set
the precedent for theatrical procedure in Moscow, has devoted months, sometimes years, to the preparation of a single
work.

The one characteristic of the Russian theatre about which
all Western stage artists have heard is the long rehearsal
period. Many of us sigh wistfully for ample time to bring a
work of art to final fruition. Actually, I wonder, even as I
wondered after my earlier exposures to the Soviet stage,
whether we would know what to do with three or four
months of rehearsal if we were granted them, whether we
could accomplish anything if we worked only three or four
hours a day over that stretch of time, and whether we could
sustain the interest of all concerned without going stale.
Temperamentally, we are quite unlike the Russians in this
respect: The long view is all-important to them; they are
accustomed to waiting. We are impatient and anxious for
immediate results; the long view holds no charm for us. This
is as true in the arts as it is in politics.

The principal artistic responsibility at the Vakhtangov
Theatre is being shouldered today by men and women of
middle age and younger. Twenty-five years ago, after looking

at Vakhtangov rehearsals, I reported that the "first thing that astonished me was [the artists'] youth. Hardly any actor seemed to be beyond thirty, some looked as though they were still in their teens." Simonov, one of those who had been with Vakhtangov from the start, was then thirty-five. His generation, which is now the old guard, is consequently between forty-five and sixty. But the Vakhtangov has seen to it that the ranks have been kept filled with new talent, and thus this theatre has avoided the weakness I have noted in the MXAT and the Maly, namely, an older and a younger but no *middle* generation. At the Vakhtangov almost all the principal roles are performed by actors between the ages of twenty-eight and forty-eight, with the older members of the company playing supporting character parts. The shining artists of this troupe —and they do indeed shine glowingly even though, technically, they are not stars—are Julia Borisova, Mikhail Ulyanov, and Yuri Yakovlev, the eldest of whom cannot be more than thirty-five.

Not all of this fortunate situation is attributable to the exigencies of the calendar. Since Vakhtangov formed his studio forty years ago, with actors then in their late teens and early twenties, its charter members are inevitably about sixty now. If that original generation had held the reins tightly in their own hands and kept all the best parts for themselves, as the MXAT appears to have done, the Vakhtangov Theatre's problem today might be comparable to that of the Art Theatre. Since they did not, it is possible to say, at the end of four decades, that the Vakhtangov seems one of the youngest theatres in Moscow.

It is natural that Vakhtangov's tradition should flourish most strongly in the theatre that bears his name; here dwells the remainder of the group with which he actually worked. Yet there are other artists in Moscow who either worked with

Vakhtangov personally or who have been strongly attracted
to the kind of theatre that stands between the extremes of
Stanislavski's devotion to inner feeling and of Meierhold's
devotion to outward form. When I left Moscow twenty-five
years ago, I called the Vakhtangov Theatre "the first representative of the theatre of the future" and said that along this
path lay the direction which a living Russian theatre must
take. Time has upheld my prediction. Today, no theatre seeks
to model itself exactly on the MXAT (not even its offshoot,
the Sovremennik) and none would faithfully follow Meierhold's suicidal path. But there are many artists who, whether
they acknowledge their debt to Vakhtangov or not, are seeking in some measure to accept Stanislavski's legacy with one
hand while grasping with the other at Vakhtangov's "maximum sharpness and definite form."

One such theatre is the Mossoviet, where, aside from the
theatre on the Arbat, the Vakhtangov tradition is at its strongest. It is only natural that this should be so, for the Mossoviet's Artistic Director, Yuri Zavadski, was one of Vakhtangov's early disciples. Like almost all of Moscow's leading
directors, he began his theatrical career as an actor. History
records that he played major roles in Vakhtangov's first productions: the role of St. Anthony in Maeterlinck's *The Mir-
acle of St. Anthony* and that of the Prince in *Princess Turandot*. By the time I reached Moscow in 1934, Zavadski had
broken away from Vakhtangov's other disciples to form his
own theatre studio, trying his wings as a *régisseur* and testing
his theories, while he simultaneously acted from time to time
at the MXAT. Later in the thirties, taking some of his studio's members with him, he assumed the Artistic Directorship
of the Theatre of the Red Army. Here he fell into disfavor,
so it is reported, and he went with his collective to Rostov,
where he worked for a number of years. Returning to Moscow
as a prodigal son, he is now one of the city's principal

theatrical leaders. Tall, distinguished-looking, and benign, with a halo of white hair around his balding pate that reminds one of Stanislavski, Zavadski leads a theatre that is notable for the excellence of its principal actors. Among the group are Lyubov Orlova, Vera Maretskaya, Nikolai Mordvinov, and Ratislav Platt; and it is their individual strength rather than the level of the ensemble that gives the theatre its stature.

Vakhtangov's principle that each play must have its own style of presentation finds full practice in Zavadski's theatre. I have described in chapter two his production of *The Merry Wives of Windsor*. *Catherine LeFèvre,* which the rest of the world knows as Victorien Sardou's *Madame Sans-Gêne,* is performed with the same bold, swashbuckling theatricality. These are in strong contrast to the group's production of Chekhov's *The Wood Demon,* that seldom-seen study from which *Uncle Vanya* subsequently evolved. *The Wood Demon* is given a performance that is simultaneously active and brooding. Played in a setting that is pastel and *en plein-air,* its action is drawn down toward the front of the Mossoviet's deep stage, with entrances below the curtain line even in the manner that Simonov was planning for the production of *Life* at the Vakhtangov. The production rings true psychologically. But it is no literal translation of life to the stage. Platt, the fine actor who enacts Yegor Petrovich Voinitski, nevertheless endows his portrait with movingly human touches, for he knows that in playing Chekhov, the actor must understand the "subtext"—what the character feels but does *not* put into words—if he is to reveal Chekhov's complete meaning.

To perform Jean-Paul Sartre's *La Putain Respecteuse* (which is called *Lizzie MacKay* in Moscow) requires no such psychological depth. Everything it means it says. It is a much more obvious theatre piece, and again the Mossoviet produc-

tion takes its style from the play—or gives to the play that
form which best suits it: violent melodrama. Tension is high
from the rise of the first curtain, never abating until the resolution—a resolution which, so Orlova who plays Lizzie told
me, has been rewritten for the Moscow version by Sartre himself, in order to provide that optimistic conclusion which the
Party line favors.

The Mossoviet Theatre's popularity is attested by its constantly sold-out houses. Its repertoire is cosmopolitan: alongside Shakespeare, Chekhov, Sardou, and Sartre, there are also
productions of Mikhail Lermontov, Carlo Goldoni, Gorki,
and Ibsen out of the past, and at least five contemporary
Soviet pieces. Before the end of the 1960–1961 season, this
company expected to present *Orpheus Descending*, the first
Tennessee Williams play ever to be presented in Moscow. In
their eagerness to present Williams' milieu correctly, they
invited me to come to a rehearsal to help them with various
problems whose solution was difficult because of their totally
different background and experience. I did my best to oblige.
But it was a difficult task, for the inhabitants and environment of a small Southern American town really have no
counterpart in Soviet life. Even if the play were produced
with exactitude, the Soviet public would find it all so exotic
and so far from their preconceptions of American mores that
I suspect it would be unacceptable. Whether Williams can
gain the popularity in the Soviet Union that Arthur Miller
and Lillian Hellman have already acquired there, let alone
the popularity he has achieved in America, strikes me as
exceedingly doubtful.

When I asked Yuri Osnos, the translator of *Orpheus Descending*, why this work had been chosen rather than the
superior *The Glass Menagerie* or *A Streetcar Named Desire*,
he replied that the former was too delicately tenuous for
Soviet taste, the latter too violent. Since *The Glass Menagerie*

strikes me as being no more delicate a work of art than *The Three Sisters* and *Streetcar* no more violent than *The Respectful Prostitute,* I can explain his judgment only by qualifications, saying that *The Three Sisters* is, after all, Russian and that the Sartre play carries a social message and can also be construed as anti-American propaganda, if one wishes to do so.

Clearly, the Mossoviet is brave to introduce Tennessee Williams into the Soviet capital at all. Zavadski, however, is a devoted promoter of cultural exchange as a means of alleviating international tensions, and this fact undoubtedly entered into his decision to show his countrymen the work of one of America's most popular dramatists. He spent six weeks in the spring of 1959 in New York, lecturing and working on rehearsals of *The Cherry Orchard* with a professional student group at the Institute for Advanced Studies in the Theatre Arts. The American theatre has no warmer advocate in Moscow than Yuri Zavadski of the Mossoviet Theatre.

8

The Way

into the Theatre

One of the most unique aspects of American theatrical life, viewed from the European's vantage point, is our academic theatre. It is no longer news that on scores of American college and university campuses there exist courses in acting, directing, stagecraft, and playwriting; departments offering master's and doctor's degrees in drama; and playhouses whose electronic, hydraulic, and other mechanical and architectural features far excel even those of Broadway. No other country in the world has anything to compare with us in educational theatre. Today, however, the chairman of almost every one of these drama departments will tell you that his department does *not* exist principally as a training ground for young people who want to become professional actors.

When I explained this to a group of students at the Maly Theatre School in Moscow, they asked the obvious question, "Where, then, does all this lead?" I explained that a majority of these hundreds of graduates go into teaching drama or into working with amateurs in community theatres. I went on to remark that the principal importance of our academic theatre, in my opinion, lies in the fact that it both directly and indirectly builds up throughout the country a public awareness of and appreciation for the living stage, without which the theatre cannot flourish.

My interlocutors pressed on with their questioning. "Where, then, does the young person of talent prepare for a professional career on the stage?"

I replied that truly professional acting schools existed principally in New York, in the Los Angeles area, and in Chicago. They were astounded when I told them, in response to further questioning, that at these professional schools—like the American Academy of Dramatic Arts, the Neighborhood Playhouse School of the Theatre, the Pasadena Playhouse College of Theatre Arts, the Goodman Memorial Theatre School of Drama in Chicago, and the school of the American Theatre Wing—the course was usually of two years' duration; and that, in addition to these schools, we had such "studios" as those of Stella Adler, Paul Mann, Herbert Berghof and Uta Hagen, where the duration of study depended entirely upon the student and not upon a fixed curriculum.

The reader perhaps may in turn be astounded by Soviet training practices. To prepare actors for the professional dramatic theatre, Moscow now has five institutions: schools attached to the three largest theatres—the Maly, the Moscow Art, and the Vakhtangov, called respectively the Shchepkin Theatrical School, the Nemirovich-Danchenko School, and the Shchukin School—a small group attached to the Central Children's Theatre; and the State Institute of Theatre Arts, called by the initials of the Russian words for this title, GITIS. Together, these schools train a total of approximately nine hundred full-time students for the various arts and crafts of the stage, though the trainees are principally

would-be actors. In other cities of the Soviet Union, there are
other theatre schools, but I presume Moscow's are the best.
(I except, as usual, the ballet schools from my generalization.
In this field, Leningrad has always been and still is supreme.)

Approximately one hundred and forty young people are
enrolled in the Shchepkin Theatrical School, which occupies
a three-story, mustard-colored building across the street from
the east façade of the Maly Theatre. The long classroom
windows that look away from the street face across a courtyard toward the Ballet School of the Bolshoi, whose practice
pianos one faintly hears across the intervening distance. I
arrived punctually at ten o'clock one morning to find school
in full session. I was ushered into the spacious office of the
school's director, a grave gentleman who, after greeting me,
summoned several of his faculty to join us. For an hour or so
we discussed education for the theatre.

The Shchepkin Theatrical School, I discovered, prefers to
accept students who have had no previous experience or
training. "That way they have no bad habits we must break,"
explained the director. Each year there are seven or eight
hundred applicants, most of them having just finished high
school and being seventeen or eighteen years old. Out of these
hundreds, only about twenty-five are selected, after a careful
screening. This screening is first accomplished by means of
interviews, during which many stagestruck youngsters are
persuaded that the theatre is not for them. Then comes a
series of three examinations, which test the candidate's ability
to read aloud intelligently, to interpret what he reads with
imagination, and to handle his body acceptably. The reading
examination is particularly important at the Shchepkin
Theatrical School, since the Maly, to which the school is
attached, is a theatre whose standard of the spoken word is
regarded as the standard for all Russia. The examiners, having taken the prospect's background of literary knowledge
into consideration, look for independence and originality of

interpretation. They look for signs of the candidate's physical or mental potentialities as a dramatic or a lyrical or a character actor. Presumably, the examiners are also seeking a heterogeneous group for each entering class, and would not be anxious to accept an entire group of, say, incipient character actors or of ingénues.

It usually turns out that when the class has been selected, the boys outnumber the girls two to one. When I remarked that this was an unusual proportion from the American dramatic school's viewpoint, I was asked why, since "most plays, both classic and modern, have more male characters than female, and an acting company must therefore be preponderately masculine." I had no ready answer, except to say that it is my impression that by and large our theatre is a more feminine institution than theirs: That on the one hand, Broadway performs few classics; while on the other hand, our contemporary plays are often written with an eye to providing a vehicle for our leading performers, a majority of whom are women.

One-third to one-half of the entering class at the Shchepkin Theatrical School comes from outside the environs of Moscow. In such cases, the newly arrived students become boarding students, living in the dormitory maintained for those who come from the provinces. If the student is a Muscovite, he will live at home, but he will probably still take two meals a day in the school's dining room. Whether he receives a stipend will depend on his family's financial resources. If its per-capita income is greater than five hundred rubles* a month, he will receive free tuition and nothing more. If its income is less than five hundred rubles, additional financial aid is provided.

The entering student begins a training program that lasts four years, twice as long as that considered needful by our

---

* All currency figures quoted to me were based on the 1960 valuation of the ruble.

American and British professional schools. How does the student spend these four years? He will devote approximately fifty-four hundred hours to classes held six days a week; and the school will, in all likelihood, commandeer his time during another three or four thousand hours, for he has homework to do, rehearsals outside class hours in which to take part, and, in the evenings, performances either on the school stage or, during his upper-class years, on the big stage of the Maly Theatre itself. Excepting the summer holidays, there is little time he can call his own.

The key course at the Shchepkin School, as at all other theatre schools, is called "Mastery of Acting." This course consumes two thousand hours. Here, as in every Russian dramatic school, the cornerstone of the course is the Stanislavski system, and a working knowledge of this system is required of every young actor. It is considered essential that the student understand what the great master stood for, that he has learned to practice what Stanislavski preached, in order to earn the right to deviate. What is built on that foundation varies from school to school, depending on the patron theatre's artistic tenets and on the extent to which these deviate from the Moscow Art Theatre. The Vakhtangov's Shchukin School, as we shall see, reflects its patron theatre's artistic line, a line which leads away from slavish practice of realism toward a brighter theatricality. The emphasis is on the mastery of outward form; thus the school provides exercises designed to achieve that mastery. At the Shchepkin, since the spoken word is prized above all things, the emphasis is more especially in this direction.

During the first semester of his first year at the Shchepkin School, the entering student's course in "Mastery of Acting" consists principally of "etudes"—in this instance, of improvisations done without words. In the second semester, he is given a novel to read, then asked to perform scenes from it. He is required to use words while enacting these scenes, but the words must be those of his own improvisation, not the author's. It is not until the second year that he first begins to work on selections from contemporary drama, then on those from various classical periods. Not until the third year do he and his classmates tackle a whole play, and even then such a project is treated as a classroom exercise. Finally, in the fourth year, he performs publicly in the school's own theatre or on the stage of the Maly's subsidiary theatre, the Maly Filial, where, in both cases, he works under a regular director, not under a teacher who treats him like a student, and where also a genuine audience will judge his work. His so-called "thesis" performance at the completion of the fourth year determines his final grade.

Most of the "Mastery of Acting" courses take place at the end of the afternoon, since at the Shchepkin Theatrical School they are conducted by leading actors and *régisseurs* of the Maly who are involved in their own rehearsals during the remainder of the day and in their own performances during the evenings. Thus, in order that I might attend my first acting class, I had to return to the school at half-past four. The distinguished gray-haired actor who was its teacher led me along a corridor and then into a small room, where about fifteen second-year students were already waiting. The youngsters stopped talking and stood up when the two of us entered. When we were seated, they sat down. Such courteous formality is the rule in all classes in every school, even to the eight-year-olds in the Bolshoi Ballet School who bow or curtsy gravely and say *"zdravstvuite"* ("How do you do") when they encounter a visitor in the halls.

Perhaps for my benefit, the class reviewed an exercise in which they pretended to be animals. One student curled up on the floor as a dog; he panted, he dozed, he hunted fleas. Two other boys and a girl then scratched about an imaginary barnyard, like two roosters and a hen; as the hen clucked vigorously, the roosters fought over her, chasing each other around the yard. Another boy followed with an admirable impersonation of a donkey. The students who formed the audience laughed till tears rolled down their cheeks.

The next exercise was a series of improvisations which involved people, not animals. The class paired off to present these invented situations, some of which were hilarious, though others were serious and frequently took a quite melodramatic turn, as in the case of one boy who threatened another's life because his girl had been taken away from him. When this exercise was completed, two of the girls at a murmured word from the instructor became involved in an argument over the notebook of one of them; the boys sitting next to them also became involved, and in no time the whole class was embroiled. Finally, one student, shouting to be heard over the noisy melee, reminded them that a visitor was present. They all looked abashed and quickly calmed down. Several smoothed back their hair, and two or three came over to apologize to the teacher and to me. But the whole incident, it turned out, was only a class exercise. There had never been any real argument. It was entirely improvised, though so effectively that I honestly thought for a while that things were getting out of hand.

There are a great many other courses which surround the "Mastery of Acting" course, and which also contribute directly to the student's stage deportment. My first morning at the school I was taken to watch a beginning class in speech. There were exercises in breath control, during which the students slowly counted up to twelve in one breath; in pronunciation of vowel and consonant combinations; in the vocal placement of the voice; and in the coördination of vocal rhythms with body movements. I visited a class in the techniques of stage movement, where second-year students were performing head, hand, arm, foot, and neck exercises evolved from dramatic situations and done in time to music.

The best way of setting forth the scope and the thoroughness of the Soviet theatre schools, which take the place of four years of college, is to present the Shchepkin Theatrical School's curriculum in toto. This is how a student spends his almost fifty-four hundred hours during the four years:

THEATRICAL COURSES	HOURS
Mastery of Acting	2,000
Stage Speech	326
Stage Movement	108
Dancing	420
Fencing	68
Musical Training	136
Solo Singing	66
Make-up	97
History of Russian Theatre	172
History of World Theatre	136
Production Practice*	400

IDEOLOGICAL COURSES	
History of Communist Party	
Political Economy	
Dialectical Materialism	450
Esthetics	

ACADEMIC COURSES	
History of Russian Literature	
History of Foreign Literature	
History of Art	1,000
Foreign Language (usually French)	

PHYSICAL EDUCATION	
Physical Culture (first year)	No specified number
Sports (after first year)	

* This course includes study of costumes and scenery, sound effects, organization, participation in mob scenes of Maly productions (beginning in the second year), and performances of bit parts in Maly productions (beginning in the third year).

It is obvious, of course, that the Shchepkin graduate has achieved nothing like a liberal arts education. He has plunged directly from high school into vocational training with but a cursory nod toward a background of general culture. As a long and warm exponent of a solid foundation in the liberal arts for the young actor, I can give only limited support to the Soviet system. Nevertheless, I am compelled to admit that when his four years are completed, a young actor is able to walk onto a stage with far greater command of the technique of his profession than is any college-trained American at the age of twenty-one or twenty-two. At the Mayakovski Theatre, for example, the title role in *Hamlet* is played by a young man named Edward Martsevich. He was awarded the part by Okhlopkov the first year after his graduation from the Shchepkin School. He was then twenty-two years old. A year later, I watched the performance of this lad, the youngest professional actor I had ever seen play this most exacting of all stage roles. His sensitive blond features and slender body were reminiscent of James Dean, but he was as manly and vigorously agile as Douglas Fairbanks, Sr., ever was. His authority, his handling of his body and voice, bore ample testimony to the thoroughness of Moscow theatrical training, for he performed like a veteran, and I could think of no graduate of any of our universities to equal him at the age of twenty-three. If the intellectual maturity one looks for in Shakespeare's profoundest and subtlest creation was not there in full measure, it is not wholly surprising. At least the technique is there today, and I suspect his interpretation will deepen in future years.

Every Shchepkin graduate is self-confident not only because of his training; he has a further confidence denied to our graduates in that he knows a job in the professional theatre actually awaits him. Three or four from each graduating class will be absorbed by the Maly into its own company.

The rest will go to other Moscow theatres, as Martsevich went to the Mayakovski, or they will go to theatres in the provinces. The point is that everyone is guaranteed a post in some theatre, and that no one's training will go for naught. There is no unemployment of actors in the Soviet Union.

GITIS, unlike the other schools I visited, is attached to no particular theatre. It is located in a big, yellow-and-white, nineteenth-century building on a back street near Arbat Square. The building looked familiar to me as I walked up its rain-drenched driveway, for I had been there twenty-five years beforehand to call on A. N. Furminova, its director, when it was called the Central Theatre Technicum. In the intervening years, however, the school has grown in size and scope, so that it now operates at university level, with a graduate school offering degrees up to and including a doctorate of fine arts. The student body numbers five hundred, together with an additional four hundred who are enrolled in what we would call "extension" courses or "adult education." Today, GITIS trains its students as actors not only for the dramatic theatre but also for musical comedy and operetta; it trains others as directors of drama and opera, as ballet masters, as teachers of choreography, and as critics. It is principally those studying to become critics who will work for their doctorates. The others complete their courses in four or five years (four years for actors, five for *régisseurs* and choreographers).

When I had visited the Central Theatre Technicum, I had been impressed by the job it was then doing in training and sending out entire theatre collectives to the outlying republics of the U.S.S.R. This program continues at GITIS but at a much reduced scale, for thirteen of the Union's sixteen autonomous republics now have their own theatrical training institutions (for example, the excellent one in Tbilisi in

Georgia). Today, at GITIS the students from Uzbekistan or from Soviet Armenia have been largely replaced by students from Bulgaria, Romania, and other satellite countries. Altogether, thirty-eight nations are represented in the school's student body, though there are no Americans because no student exchanges have been effected in this field, a fact which I consider regrettable.

It is as difficult to secure admission to GITIS as to any other theatre school, for there are twenty applicants for every vacancy. I was told that more girls apply for admission than do boys. Yet the fact remains that more boys than girls are accepted, so that out of a class of twenty-five, the ratio will be approximately sixteen to nine. Fifteen to twenty students are annually accepted into the course for *régisseurs*, twenty-five into the acting course, another twenty-five into the musical operetta course. Fifteen to twenty enter the program for critics, and approximately twenty-five come each year to form a studio group from one or another of the outlying republics. Applicants for the acting course need not be more than seventeen years old; but those who enroll in the courses for *régisseurs*, choreographers, and critics are usually twenty years of age, for it is considered desirable that they should have spent two years at some job after leaving high school, preferably with an amateur theatre. All students at GITIS receive stipends, but, for the youths of outstanding talent, special scholarships amounting to as much as six or eight hundred rubles a month are provided.

Here, as at most Soviet theatre schools, the entering student is on probation for his first two years, his talent for the stage being given that length of time to assert itself. If it becomes evident during this period that the student's gifts are too limited or that his personality is not suitable for a dramatic career, he is asked to leave at a time when, being no more than twenty or so, he still has time to develop an interest in another profession. If he remains after the two-year period, he is practically certain of graduating and of being provided thereafter with a job in his own area of theatrical specialization.

The curriculum follows the basic line I have already detailed for the Shchepkin School, certain adjustments naturally being made to fit the needs of the special fields involved. But since GITIS is dependent on no one theatre and so tends to lack the intimate relationships to a functioning company—such as the Shchepkin, the Shchukin, and the Nemirovich-Danchenko Schools enjoy—a compensatory program is developed under which, beginning in the third year, students are assigned to work in various Moscow theatres on a part-time basis, in addition to the regularly assigned roles in the Institute's own theatre. In this latter theatre, a student of acting is assured of playing at least twenty or thirty roles during his four years' course, most of them in performances which are open to the general public at a low admission. In addition, the student *régisseurs* are expected to stage a play either at some theatre in Moscow or at one in the provinces during their fifth year, thus completing their "thesis" requirements.

One of the most extraordinary things about GITIS is the enormous size of its faculty. There is, I was told, one teacher for every two students! The acting department alone has a hundred instructors. Though only a few of these devote their full time to the institute, most of them come at least two or three times a week for a four-hour session. Through this arrangement, the GITIS student is brought into classroom contact with some of the masters of the Moscow theatre world, among them Zavadski of the Mossoviet, V. A. Orlov and I. M. Raevski of the Art Theatre, and Maria Knebel of the Central Children's Theatre. This sense of responsibility which the older generation in the Russian theatre feels toward its juniors is one of its major strengths. Men and women who lead far busier professional lives in their repertory theatres than do most of our own established artists pour out vast quantities of time and energy teaching the young what they themselves have learned, not only in classrooms but also at seminars and discussions (conducted under the auspices of the All-Russian Theatrical Society) that often continue until the small hours of the morning. From the moment the neophyte artist of seventeen or eighteen is accepted into a theatre school, he is made to feel part of the profession. There is none of the segregation of apprentice from master, of the educational from the professional world that unfortunately characterizes our theatre in the United States and that creates, in effect, two worlds uneasily tangential to one another.

It is in the field of stagecraft where much of the best training is provided in the American educational theatre. There are courses in scene design, in costume design, and in the techniques of lighting. In this kind of training we are far ahead of the Russians. The Soviet curricula I have described put little emphasis on this side of theatre because, of course, the Soviet schools are essentially oriented to the training of actors. But there are two outstanding technical programs in the U.S.S.R., one in Leningrad at the school attached to the Theatre of Comedy, directed by Nikolai Akimov, the other a department of the Nemirovich-Danchenko School of the Moscow Art Theatre. The latter is under the direction of Vadim Shverobovich, who has been the Technical Director of the MXAT for a number of years and who is the son of none other than the great Art Theatre actor, Kachalov. Since Akimov is one of the Soviet Union's leading stage designers, it is natural that his school should excel as a school for designers; since Shverobovich is a technician, his courses understandably emphasize stagecraft.

Shverobovich's department at the Nemirovich-Danchenko
School is new and very nearly unique. It was founded in 1959.
In 1960, there were thirty-five students. By now, there should
be approximately seventy-five students majoring in the four-
year course in stagecraft. The students are given courses in
mechanical stage equipment, lighting, scenery and property
building, costume design and construction, stage effects
(which, I gather, means largely sound), in theatrical radio, in
painting and freehand drawing, and in the history of the
graphic arts. There are, in addition, the usual courses in the
history of the theatre, both Russian and foreign; the history
of literature; a course in one foreign language; and, last but
not least, a survey course entitled "Creation of External
Forms of Stage Production," which seems to sum up almost
every course offered by the department.

Twenty-five years ago I characterized the technical side of
the Soviet theatre as "brave in conception, weak in execution." Today, the Nemirovich-Danchenko School may be taking the first step toward making a change.

The students at the Vakhtangov's Shchukin School are in
love with the theatre. Not that students elsewhere are not in-
fatuated, but at the Shchukin there seems to be an enthusiasm which sweeps far more exuberantly through every
classroom than is the case at the Maly's Shchepkin School.
Tradition and formality, which mean so much to the Maly in
maintaining its position as Moscow's Comédie Française, are
alien to the Shchukin. Perhaps it is partly that the youngsters
here have already acquired some of the Vakhtangov Theatre's
bright spirit and its tendency to look at the playhouse as truly
a house for play. In any event, there can be no doubt that a
more relaxed attitude, a camaraderie exists between instructors and their charges at the Shchukin.

The school claims to be older than the theatre which

sponsors it, for it considers its genesis to have been in the lectures that Vakhtangov began delivering forty-six years ago, or seven years before his theatre came into full-fledged being. In 1939, the school became the Shchukin School in honor of Boris Shchukin, one of the Vakhtangov's greatest actors. Today Boris Zakhava, the former Artistic Director of the Vakhtangov Theatre, is the school's head.

Much of what I have reported about the Shchepkin School applies also to the Shchukin School. There are approximately the same number of students, who are of the same age, have passed the same entrance requirements, and are involved in the same curriculum. It is in the "Mastery of Acting" courses that a difference is to be noted, and even then it is not until the second year, when the student has passed through the standard "etude" phase, that this difference becomes readily apparent. At this point the Shchukin students begin studies in the creation of "stage images": They go out into the streets to watch the passers-by; they are assigned to factory benches, to barber shops, to restaurant kitchens, to hospitals, and to dozens of other places to observe people at work. The results of their observations are brought back to the classroom.

No classroom exercise which I attended in Moscow was more engrossing. A succession of carefully captured images was paraded before us, each so accurate in its outward details that one forgot where one was and that this was make-believe. We saw students impersonating men of varying ages and occupations walking down the street, and by their gait and outward mien it was possible to recognize each type. We saw a man sitting at the theatre absorbed in watching a play. We saw a boy and his girl leaning over a gallery rail watching another performance, yet simultaneously preoccupied with each other. We observed one boy turn himself into a tailor expertly snipping and measuring, another into a dyer moving with ease among his vats, a third into a pharmacist preparing a prescription, a fourth into an orchestra conductor at a rehearsal. There was no dramatic situation involved, no psychological conflict. The results were entirely those of the visual observation that is an essential means for achieving the Vakhtangov's basic esthetic aim: the wedding of outward form to inner truth. It is within this framework that the students at the Shchukin, in contrast to those at the Maly, are asked to select scenes from modern novels and adapt them to the stage. At examination time this framework is extended further: A student is frequently asked to play a scene based on a novel on which he has worked, but a scene that is not in the original.

One of my most agreeable hours at the Shchukin School was spent in a class which, for want of a better name, I might call a session in "musical images." A group of students, singly or in pairs, stood in front of a screen and performed vocal solos or duets, piano selections, or violin pieces. The point was that no one was actually making music. The pianist was playing on a table; the violinist had only two sticks, using the one as a bow, the other as his fiddle; the singer only mouthed the words. All the actual sounds came from behind the screen, where other students were doing the singing and playing. But such accurate "dubbing" was accomplished that one was almost sure the music was coming from the table or the two sticks or the open mouths of the "singers." The students were delighted at my amazement, and would have been glad to go on performing indefinitely.

So impressed was I by the Shchukin School that, at the end of a fourth-year class which was rehearsing for a public presentation of Molière's *Le Bourgeois Gentilhomme,* I told the Vakhtangov actor who was directing that the performance I had just witnessed was as good as any I had seen on a Moscow stage. In retrospect, I still agree with that judgment not only about the performance but about the entire school as

well. The Molière production was being done as Molière had
ordered—as a comedy ballet. The young people who capered
and pirouetted in their sports shirts and sweaters, their knee-
length skirts and twentieth-century trousers, forced one to
forget these habiliments of rehearsal and to fancy oneself
transported back three hundred years. In its student M. Jourdain, this production had a comedian who was every bit as
funny as the late Bobby Clark, the last Jourdain I had seen.
If the Shchukin actors, none of them over twenty-two, can be
that finished and witty in the performance of what we in
America consider very difficult stuff indeed—namely, Molière—then surely the acting standards of Moscow's theatres
are safely high enough for at least another generation.

9

Production

Notes

"Do not reproach me for my contradictions," wrote the Marquis de Custine in his *Journals,* recounting his visit to Russia in 1839. ". . . they exist in the things that I describe—let this be said once and for all." In a later passage, the French traveler reported, "Endowed with little ingenuity, [the Russians] usually lack machinery for the end they wish to achieve. The Russians are the Romans of the North. Both have taken their sciences and their arts from foreign lands. . . . Theirs is an imitative mind . . . it copies everything and creates nothing. . . ."

At no time do the Marquis de Custine's observations, both with regard to contradictions and the Russians in general, seem more sound than when one turns to the paradox of the Russian theatre in its physical aspects. Russian architecture is derivative, yet simultaneously extremely serviceable; scene design is currently barren; stage mechanics are far behind the Western world's (especially Germany's and America's); their costuming is both good and bad; yet, finally, Russian make-up and sound effects are superb.

I suppose it ill behooves a man coming from New York to complain that there is little of interest in theatrical architecture in Moscow. No new legitimate playhouse has been built in our own theatrical capital since 1928, and even the one built then was based on concepts that had already been established for twenty years. Thus, all Broadway theatres are fifty years behind the times, whereas the Muscovites can exhibit six that have been erected or rebuilt in the last thirty years: the Kamerny (now the Pushkin), the Vakhtangov, Central Theatre of the Soviet Army, the Kremlin Theatre, the Mossoviet, and the Stanislavski-Nemirovich-Danchenko Musical Theatre. (One of these, the Vakhtangov, is a replacement of an earlier building on the same site which was destroyed by a World War II bomb.) Yet, it remains true that if one comes to the Russian theatrical capital from Germany or from a tour of American universities or with the plans for New York's new Lincoln Center for the Performing Arts in mind, one is bound to say that the Russians are behind the times. They have contributed nothing new in recent years in the fields of theatrical architecture or of stage mechanics. The theatres of Moscow may once have been better than those of New York, but, despite their head start, the Russians have failed to make additional experiments and advances.

Even the exteriors of Moscow's new theatres are not remarkable. None has the early nineteenth-century elegance of the old Bolshoi or Maly. Contemporary Soviet architecture is tasteless and heavy, adorned with too much marble and statuary to please Western eyes. The theatres of Moscow possess the same facelessness as the surrounding new buildings. The Mossoviet's largely glass façade is certainly the most modern and dramatic in town, but it suffers by being hidden in the rear corner of a little park, with a rather disreputable motion-picture theatre en face. The huge Central Theatre of the Soviet Army, on the other hand, has the advantage of a commanding site, isolated and facing a public square, but its situation only serves to call attention to the heavy gracelessness of this modern adaptation of Russian neoclassical architecture. This theatre is the showplace among Moscow playhouses, notwithstanding. Erected in 1940 and designed in the shape of a five-pointed star, it actually contains two theatres, an intimate one seating six hundred and a larger hall that seats two thousand. By far the most impressive thing about the larger theatre is the spatial relationship of the stage to the auditorium. The latter is dwarfed by the immensity of the backstage space. From the proscenium, which is ninety-eight feet wide, the stage stretches back one hundred and ninety-six feet. Standing in the center of this stage is like standing in the middle of a prairie. Looking up, one's gaze travels seventy-five feet to the gridiron under the roof. Under one's feet is a turntable that is one hundred and five feet in diameter. A smaller turntable, forty-nine feet in diameter, within the large one can be operated independently. In other words, while the big one revolves slowly clockwise, the little one can be revolving more rapidly counterclockwise, or vice versa. In addition, the big turntable is divided into rectangular sections that can be raised or sunk by hydraulic action to as much as eleven feet above or below stage level. Offstage, there are dressing-room facilities for a cast of one hundred.

Yet the only really remarkable thing about all this equipment is that it is designed for a dramatic theatre seating two thousand. Actually, Radio City Music Hall in New York was provided with comparable facilities almost thirty years ago, but it seats over six thousand spectators. Turntables and hydraulic lifts are nothing new, yet one must salute the Russians for providing such equipment in a theatre that is dedicated to the drama only.

The legitimate theatres of Moscow remain superior to those of New York in only two ways: they are equipped with their own workshops and warehouses and they are more spacious. The workshops and warehouses are frequently in the playhouse itself or else immediately adjoining it. True, such an advantage is admittedly more important to the Russian type of operation than it is to our own, for a large number of productions play concurrently in repertory and several new productions are mounted each season by the same company, and thus the propinquity of shop and storehouse is essential. Nevertheless, in New York, too, every Broadway manager's budget would be somewhat reduced if the costly item of hauling could be eliminated, and some of the thousands of dollars spent on building and painting scenery might be saved if this work could be done within the theatre leased for a presentation.

It has already been mentioned that, almost without exception, Moscow's theatres provide proportionally more space for the audience as well as for production back stage, although seldom, with as spectacular a stage as at the Central Theatre of the Soviet Army. Anyone who has attended a play at New York's newest theatre, the Ethel Barrymore on west Forty-seventh Street, which was built in 1928, recalls its ten-by-thirty-foot lobby, which can comfortably accommodate no more than one-tenth of the theatre's possible one thousand spectators for an entr'acte cigarette. And any man who has fought his way to the tiny orangeade-and-candy stand hidden in a crowded corner at the rear of a Broadway orchestra floor would be bound to be impressed by the wide, colonnaded foyers of the Maly Theatre and particularly by its buffet, where he could purchase refreshments from three different counters and choose a seat at one of at least twenty little tables. Far more important, however, any designer or director who has had to crowd his play onto the stage of the Ethel

Barrymore, which is twenty-eight feet deep and has but twelve feet of offstage space on one side, cannot fail to be envious of the incredible sixty-three foot depth of the Moscow Art Theatre, and of its revolving stage that is fifty-five feet in diameter. New York theatres seem to have been designed to provide the maximum inconvenience and discomfort for their patrons and the minimum space for their stage technicians—the result of the high cost of real estate in the Broadway district, together with the commercial desire to devote every possible square foot of that precious space to seating the largest possible number of customers.

The Moscow theatre architects, on the other hand, have been limited by no such handicaps either before or after the Revolution. Not only do technicians and audiences fare better there, but the performers also. Dressing rooms in most Broadway theatres were miserable cells until the City Investing Company acquired half-a-dozen playhouses in the Times Square district several years ago and did a major renovating job, whereupon one or two other theatre owners followed suit. But the Moscow actor still has more room, more air, more conveniences than his American colleague. In most theatres, furthermore, he can follow the onstage action through a loudspeaker in his dressing room if he wishes; otherwise he can repair to the actors' greenroom, adjoining the stage, and mingle in comfort with his fellow players until his entrance cue comes. By contrast, New York actors must await their entrances while perched on rickety chairs set in drafty offstage wings or perhaps be pushed about by stagehands who are making quick changes.

With all this space, however, the Russians have not utilized it well. The *"décor* of the Moscow stage is brave in conception, weak in execution," I declared after taking my first long look at it in the 1930's. Today the second—and negative—

part of the judgment stands, but the first—and positive—part does not. In conception, the Moscow theatre has become less brave. There is a lack of fresh air in Russia. One has only to go from Moscow to Warsaw, as I did at the end of November, 1960, to have Soviet stage decoration put into proper perspective. The Poles have invested their productions with scenery that has wit, imagination, elegance, simplicity, high style— all words I find it impossible to apply to ninety per cent of the Soviet output. The Poles, however, look to Paris and New York for inspiration, as the Russians are not allowed to do— and then the Poles *create*. At the moment, for example, the Poles are in love with abstract art—a phenomenon which the Russians are rarely able to see.

Looking back over the approximately sixty Moscow productions I witnessed in 1960, I remember only ten whose settings were either ravishingly beautiful or arrestingly exciting, and four of these were at the State Puppet Theatre of Obraztsov. The other six were distributed among the Moscow Art Theatre, the Maly, the Vakhtangov, and the Mossoviet, and were the work of B. R. Erdman, V. F. Ryndin, I. G. Sumbatashvili (a Georgian), A. P. Vasiliev, and M. S. Saryan (an Armenian). If all these productions constituted a fair cross section of the times, then the two most active designers were Vasiliev, who designed the settings for *The Living Corpse, Catherine Le Fevre, The Wood Demon,* and *Son of the Century;* and Ryndin, who was responsible for the decor of *Vanity Fair, Hamlet, A Winter's Tale,* and the operatic version of *Mother.*

Furthermore, if these sixty or so productions were indeed a fair cross section, it is necessary for me to draw a comparison between the 1930's and the 1960's. One reason for the unfavorable contrast between Soviet stage sets of today and the thirties lies in the fact that so many of the Soviet ideas of stage design in those earlier days have been influencing the rest of the world's theatres ever since; thus they have now come to look commonplace. Furthermore, the rest of the world, having assimilated those ideas, has moved on. Taste has changed in the West. Realism and constructivism, equally, have ceased to amaze or to charm, but the Russian designers repeat themselves because they do not know what else to do. Isaac Rabinovich, for example, was one of the designers of the thirties whose work I most admired. Today, he is almost unrepresented on the Moscow stage; his setting of *The Idiot* at the Vakhtangov was the only example of his work I saw, and it consisted of—commonplace, realistic interiors and exteriors without style or originality, yet he showed both qualities in his work of the 1930's. The fact is that he, like his colleagues, has had to settle for socialist realism.

Then, too, Moscow's tradition of the continuing relationship between artist and theatre has never extended to designers, only to actors and directors, and the lack of this tradition has not been beneficial. The designers are free-lance workers who must be prepared to offer their services to any theatre that will engage them for a specific production. So it is that Ryndin designs for the Maly, the MXAT, the Mayakovski, and the Bolshoi; and that Vasiliev also works at the Maly and at the Mossoviet and the Gogol. This eclecticism in design is illustrated by the fact that at the Vakhtangov I saw the work of seven designers, although I attended but eight different productions. At the Maly and the MXAT, at each of which I also saw eight plays, five different designers were represented on each stage. Only at the Theatre of Comedy in Leningrad is there complete unity between design and direction, and this is because both are handled by the same man, Nikolai Akimov. I fail to understand why the value of a permanent creative relationship between director and designer is not acknowledged in Moscow to have the same value as the relationship between directors and actors, for, as a result of the present practice, no clear visual stylistic image emerges for any one theatre. In general, there are brighter colors and sharper lines at the Mossoviet and Vakhtangov theatres than elsewhere; and there is more monumental decoration at the MXAT and the Maly, irrespective of who has designed the scenery. Yet beyond this, it is impossible even to generalize.

It is not only that the designs on the stages of today's Moscow theatres are static. This applies to the execution of those designs as well. The painting of the sets is usually flat and lacking in texture. The carpentry job is slipshod. Doors do not hang squarely. Joints do not fit snugly. Canvas is not stretched tautly. Moldings are sometimes crooked. Only the Moscow Art Theatre and the Maly Theatre are exceptions to this rule. Their productions are beautifully built, handsomely painted, and kept in shipshape condition. The same is true of the Bolshoi Opera productions. But one must remember that these three houses are subsidized by the state; the others have to balance their budgets, and the making and maintaining of the scenery seems to be the area in which they try to save kopeks.

The battered look of the settings in most theatres is due, at least partially, to the repertory system of Soviet theatre. In repertory, the big pieces of stage scenery must be brought out of storage, set up for a performance, then struck, and returned to the warehouse. A week or so later, the entire process is repeated. Thus there is far more wear and tear on stage settings than is the case in our long-run system, in which the scenery for a one-set play may remain standing onstage untouched for a year or more. Furthermore, since Moscow productions frequently remain in a theatre's repertoire with the same scenery from five to forty years, it is no wonder that it looks the worse for wear long before it is discarded.

Another reason the scenery so often and so obviously displays its blemishes lies in the Soviet use of stage lighting, employing antediluvian techniques equally lacking in both electronic controls and poetry. The Russians seem to be unaware that an artist can truly paint with light in today's theatre. The Poles, who frequently place much less scenery on their stages than do the Russians, attain some of their most stunning effects by means of color of light and chiaroscuro. Only in its use of projections is Russian lighting superior to ours. Some of the handsomest stage effects I saw in Moscow—for *An Irkutsk Story* at the Vakhtangov, for *A Winter's Tale* at the MXAT, for *The Bedbug* at the Satire, for *The Wood Demon* at the Mossoviet—were accomplished in this way. Cranes and derricks looming through the mist, clouds scudding across the moon, abstract shapes dissolving in space, delicate birch trees glistening in the sun—all these were projected on backdrops.

Chiefly, however, the Russians continue to use stage light principally for illumination. Naturally, such a method has its advantages: for example, there is certainly no difficulty about visibility. Follow spots operated from side boxes provide an itinerant halo of brightness that chases each principal actor wherever he goes onstage. But such a method also has its disadvantages, and the chief of these is a decided lack of subtlety. I dare say few in the audience at the original American production of *A Streetcar Named Desire* were aware, for instance, that Blanche DuBois was constantly kept in a moving beam of light by Jo Mielziner, designer of the Broadway production, for the color and intensity of the beam were so subtle that the character seemed almost to radiate her own aura. The sharp circles of moving light created by the Russians' old-fashioned instruments are very distracting. This

is doubly deplorable when one considers that even the most
modest Moscow company seems to be able to afford from
two to four follow-spot operators, since manpower comes
cheap in the Soviet theatre. American designers can afford
such luxuries far less, for a special spot operator in New York
requires a minimum wage of one hundred and thirty-five dollars per week.

   With such widespread use of front lighting, less onstage
equipment is needed in Soviet theatres. General illumination
is provided by footlights and by border floodlighting from
above. Apparently, the Russians have not yet become acquainted with the Fresnel, or soft-edged spotlight. Color is
employed by a sort of primitive shorthand: white light for
daytime, blue for night, orange for lamplight or firelight. I
dare say Soviet color media number not more than ten;
whereas, by contrast, our American standard color charts
offer a selection of about seventy-five different shades and
tints with which the designer can effect any nuance he pleases,
from "chocolate" to "bastard amber."

   Paradoxically, although the Russians are on the whole inferior in their ability to light the stage, they are masters of
sound effects, of exactitude in costuming, and of the art of
make-up. The rainstorm in the second act of *Uncle Vanya*
at the Moscow Art Theatre, for instance, is unforgettable, as
one sound effect follows another. It is a summer evening, and
the windows are open. Then a breeze springs up and the
curtains start to blow. In the distance, low thunder rolls
around the horizon. A few raindrops falls. The wind quickens.
One can hear a shutter banging somewhere. Now the rain can
be heard, pouring heavily. Lightning crackles, and the claps of
thunder come one on top of another, though always timed
with such precision that no line of dialogue is muffled. But it
is only a summer thunderstorm. Soon the rain slows down,

the thunder and wind diminish. Now, one can hear the dripping from the eaves. Then there is silence.

Here was the most masterful simulation of natural sounds I have ever heard on the stage. Doubtless because of the domination of realism, the Russians are generous in their infusion of wind, of bird calls, horses' hoofs, cannon fire, distant band music, passing wagons, splashing waves. Whether or not the script calls for sound, the Russians usually supply it to good effect. And music, too, is used lavishly in their dramatic productions. All Russian theatres—perhaps again because labor costs are less of a problem in Moscow—maintain orchestras, some of these numbering as many as twenty or twenty-five pieces. In addition, the Maly also has a choral ensemble. In our legitimate dramatic productions, music is such a luxury—since its cost is so enormous—that it is never used unless it is essential to the action. But this is our loss, for one learns in Moscow how much a haunting little theme can enhance a mood, how effectively a sharp orchestral comment can be used to get a laugh, how the right music can heighten tension, stir emotion, identify characters, induce lyrical reflection, broaden the scale of the action and give it epic dimensions.

More than half the plays I saw in Moscow were costume pieces. They ranged from the Elizabethan garb of *The Merry Wives of Windsor* and *Hamlet* and *A Winter's Tale* and *Maria Stuart* to the early twentieth-century apparel of *The Twelfth Hour* and *The Bedbug*. Thus, I am in a position to say that in costuming the Russians are strong in execution. Historical periods are meticulously studied, materials are carefully selected, no expense is spared when grandeur is required; the resultant effect is substantial and authentic. Conversely, it should be said that the Russians are certainly also masters at recreating squalor on the stage. When beggars

and pilgrims wander onto the scene, it is hard to believe that
the rags they wear are not actually mud-stained, their caked
and scraggly beards really lice-ridden.

Yet, despite the excellence of individual costumes, the impression of the entire ensemble is that no mastermind has
designed the whole. Colors often clash, and there is seldom a
dominant scheme. The overriding style that Cecil Beaton,
Alvin Colt, or Lucinda Ballard impart to a production is
lacking. It is as though the cast had been invited to one of
those costume parties where one is told to "come as your
favorite character"—out of Chekhov, let us say, when everyone has gone to a fine seamstress or tailor or to a rental shop
and acquired the appropriate costume, each on his own. Every
actor's costume becomes him, and he wears it well, which is
more than our actors often know how to do; but each bears
little relationship to the others. This is another reason why
the Polish theatre, like our own, makes a more handsome
effect than does the Soviet theatre: In Warsaw, the costumes
for a play are clearly designed for ensemble effect, and with
the scenery in mind as well.

In the art of make-up, however, the Russians have always
been and still are absolute masters. From the youngest actors
of the Sovremennik to the senior members of the Moscow
Art Theatre, every performer on Moscow's stages knows exactly how to transform himself into the perfect visual image
of his role. Most of the time, in keeping with the realistic
tone, these transformations are so carefully literal that one
finds it hard to believe that the toothless old porter with the
pockmarked face and the stringy white hair is a decent-look-
ing young man of thirty-five, that the bosomy matron with
cherry-colored cheeks and frizzled golden hair is really the
slender young brunette one met at the American Embassy
reception. And, when the need is for exaggeration or caricature or fantasy—as in *The Merry Wives of Windsor, The*

Ladies and the Hussars, or *The Naked King*—the Russians can, with equal deftness, create noses of just the right size, shape, and color to make the point; they can arch or slant eyebrows at a perfect angle; and they can don upswept or down-sagging mustachios that are hilariously preposterous.

If it seems strange that the Russians can create a breath-taking thunderstorm while at the same time allowing the door of a stage set to quake like an aspen, when slammed by an exiting *paterfamilias,* that they can show no sense of style in a collection of costumes, but infinite good style in a collection of make-ups; that they can make a fire blaze on a hearth with utter credibility, yet fool no one about the moonlight that streams so brightly blue through the windows—if, I say, this seems inconsistent, then I have succeeded in my portrayal of Russian technical practices. For there is here no standard of excellence that obtains equally through all the crafts of theatre. There is no rhyme nor reason.

10

Artists

Offstage

On an evening in early October, 1960, I sat at the Moscow Art
Theatre watching a performance of *The Cherry Orchard*. A
cough, the persistent remnant of a cold contracted a few
weeks earlier, troubled me during the third act. At the intermission, a rather heavy-set, blowsy, middle-aged woman sitting next to me turned and offered me a lemon drop from a
box of candy she had in her lap. "It will ease your throat,"
she said. I thanked her, and we started a desultory conversation in Russian, out of which emerged the fact that I worked
in the American theatre.

Her face lit up. "I work in the theatre, too," she said. "My
name is Natalia Sats."

I stared at her, stunned. My mind went back to a luncheon
at the American Embassy twenty-six years earlier, when
Ambassador William Bullitt had seated me next to the chic
and charming young lady who ran the Theatre for Children
in Moscow. Her father had been the musical director and
principal composer of the Moscow Art Theatre.

"It's not possible," I said. "You're dead!"

She laughed heartily. "What do you mean—not possible? I'm here!"

"But," I persisted, "everybody in the West thinks you're dead."

"I was away for a long time," she replied. Then she paused. After a moment she said, animatedly, "I've just come from Romania, from a conference of children's theatre workers. I used to direct the Theatre for Children here. I founded it."

"I know that very well," I replied; and told her of the many times I had been to her theatre, of the talks we had had, of what I had written in America of her work.

"Ah yes, I begin to remember you," she said. "Twenty-five years—a long time. What has happened to Ambassador Bullitt? And to Charlie Thayer?"

The lights began to lower for the last act. When it was over, she turned to me.

"Take my telephone number and call me someday soon," she said. As I wrote it down, she went on, "I must tell you about my plans. I am going to start a musical theatre for children. That's something we don't have here. Do you have such a thing in America?"

As we shook hands, I sought in her heavy face to find some vestige of the slender, smiling girl with bobbed hair I remembered. Perhaps it was discernible in the smile and the brightness of her eyes. I could not be sure.

I told a theatrical friend of this chance meeting and of Natalia Sats's altered appearance.

"Yes, Natalia Sats is back," he said. "I'd heard so. Eighteen years she was in exile. Such a life makes most women careless of their looks." Then he changed the subject.

The weeks passed and I did not call the number she had given me, although it stared up at me whenever I leafed through my address book. Somehow I felt shy about pursuing her. Then, on the eve of my departure, Natalia Sats called me.

"I hear you're about to leave. I would so like to see you before you go. May I call at your hotel tomorrow afternoon?"

Of course I said yes, amazed at her temerity. People who had been through what she had experienced would have learned to be more discreet, I thought.

At five o'clock the next day, she appeared. After divesting herself of her big black coat and fur hat and shaking out her hair in a gesture that seemed somehow familiar, she sat down and said, "Let me tell you what I have in mind. I have written my memoirs. They are going to be published in Moscow at the end of this month. I have been thinking about what you told me—that everyone in the West thinks I am dead. That is not good. If my book could be published there, people would find out I am still alive. Will you help me find a publisher?"

This so understandable desire to establish her existence to the world, after those years of proscription, moved me deeply. "Let me do what I can," I said.

"It will be an interesting book, I promise you," she continued. "Did you know, for instance, that I was staging opera at the Berlin State Opera with Otto Klemperer before I was twenty-five? I've known so many interesting people in my life—well worth writing about. For instance, look at this."

She reached into her capacious handbag and pulled out a snapshot of two young men and a girl. The laughing girl in the center with an arm around each of the men was she, the Natalia Sats of a quarter-century ago. I recognized her at once. And the two men, though twenty-five years younger, too, I recognized also. The one on the left was Anastas Mikoyan, the one on the right Nikita Khrushchev.

This anecdote serves to illustrate, it seems to me, several points about the position and life of the artist in the Soviet Union. First, of course, it provides an admirable example of the "thaw" that has taken place since Stalin's death. For what reason the government saw fit to interrupt the exceedingly valuable work Natalia Sats was doing in 1937, by sending her to Siberia, I do not know. It has been rumored that she had married Marshal Mikhail Tukhachevski, who was executed for treason in the great Stalinist purge of the Red Army in 1937–1938; and that, along with the innocent relatives of all the victims of that purge, she was sent into oblivion. Now, however, no matter what the reason for her exile, she is back, and the clear implication is that Stalin's successor is personally responsible.

Though one must certainly bear in mind that the relationship of a Soviet artist to his government can be most frightening, as in the case of Natalia Sats, the snapshot of her with Mikoyan and Khrushchev, their arms around each other, is nevertheless symbolic of the respect and eminence which the artist commands and occupies in Russia. This was true when the picture was taken, before 1937; it is still true today. Both government officials and artists are recognized members of an elite. They may be equated with the "intelligentsia," to whom Wright Miller refers, in his *Russians As People,* as "persons who earn by their occupation, their income, and their way of life a public respect which makes them the leaders of Soviet society." Together with the high government officials and performing artists, this elite minority also includes journalists, architects, painters, writers, professors, scientists, engineers, doctors, and leading technicians in many fields.

The minute Natalia Sats was reinstated, she automatically and, I assume, unconsciously resumed the prerogatives of preferred status. That was why she thought nothing of telephoning to me, a foreigner, at my hotel; why she had not hesitated, as most Russians would have done, to call upon me there; why she was in a position to act as hostess at a costly five-course dinner given for me as a farewell to a few friends in a private dining room at Moscow's most elegant restaurant, the Praga.

The inclusion of performing artists among Russia's elite, the fact that they are looked up to and honored even by their fellows among the "intelligentsia," has undoubtedly colored my opinion of the Soviet Union. For, frankly, I have not been brought up in a country where this is true. In America, people who are in the field of the performing arts, excepting perhaps the biggest Hollywood stars, are accustomed to find ing themselves, so to speak, seated below the salt. They are accustomed to being viewed with amused condescension, to being regarded as knowing little about politics or business or education or sport, and to being looked upon also in some ill-defined—and is it slightly envious—way as libertines or as very direct descendants of Nell Gwyn. In short, actors and other theatre folk are accustomed to being regarded as a some-what improper breed, living apart from and a little beneath the great majority of people, who earn their livings in more respectable fashion.

On Gorki Street, out near Pushkin Square, stands the "Dom Aktyorov," the House of Actors. This is the head-quarters and clubhouse of the All-Russian Theatrical Society, generally known by its initials as V.T.O. The organization is a cross between The Lambs club and the Actors Equity Association in New York City. It resembles the former in that through its clubhouse it provides a social gathering place where theatrical professionals may meet for a meal and a drink (the food is excellent and inexpensive), listen to a lecture, read a book in the library, look at an exhibition of, say, stage designs in the gallery, or attend a reception for a visiting fireman. It resembles Actors Equity in that the only restriction on membership is that one must have a pro-fessional connection with the theatre.

The House of Actors is a good place to frequent, if one wishes to become acquainted with Russian theatre folk off-stage and away from the rehearsal hall. I went there frequently when I was in Moscow. I was taken there by leading *régisseurs* for dinners and after-theatre suppers. I was also invited there to a reception marking the publication of a new theatre book, as well as to an exhibit of drawings by students of stage design from the Moscow Art Theatre's school. In one of the building's meeting rooms, I spoke one afternoon on the subject of the American theatre to a group of about a hundred members and guests. In one of its committee rooms, I received my official welcome to Moscow from a group of six or eight top-flight theatrical leaders, who were speaking in behalf of their colleagues. On that occasion, we sat around a table laden with pastries, fresh fruit, candy, and little cups of black coffee, as I heard accounts of the twenty-year creative famine they had suffered, as well as expressions of gratification at the subsequent "thaw" and of confidence in the future.

There are chapters of this All-Russian Theatrical Society throughout the U.S.S.R., each providing not only a gathering place for sociability, but also a forum for the exchange of ideas. Lectures, debates, and classes sponsored by V.T.O. are perhaps the most important of their functions. In Moscow, such events enable mature artists, outstanding leaders, and youthful neophytes, working in all of Moscow's twenty-five theatres, not only to become acquainted with each other but to partake in a give-and-take of criticism, in an exploration of creative ideas, in arguments over esthetic principles that make an important contribution to the ferment one feels in Moscow's artistic life. We have nothing like this organization in the American professional theatre, and it is our loss.

More relaxing and more revealing than a meeting in a semi-public place, such as the House of Actors, is a visit to an individual's house. Because few foreigners receive invitations into private homes in Moscow, let me tell you about two Sundays in October when I visited theatre people, once in town and once in the country. They reveal the artist's life offstage in a detail which I could not otherwise provide. Since I am sure both invitations were known to the Soviet authorities, I have no compunction about naming names.

"Come to dinner on Sunday at my apartment," said Reuben Nikolayevich Simonov, Artistic Director of the Vakhtangov Theatre, an old friend of twenty-five years' standing.

I accepted with pleasure.

"I shall have the car pick you up at your hotel at two o'clock," he said.

I was ready and downstairs at the appointed hour. Thirty minutes later, a blue sedan drove up. Reuben Nikolayevich was seated next to the driver.

"I'm sorry to have kept you waiting," he said, "but I've been at the Bolshoi at a conference. I am staging their new production of *Faust,* and the meeting set for noon lasted longer than I had expected."

I assured him it mattered not at all, and refrained from adding that I was only surprised he had such a good excuse and had not kept me waiting longer, for the Russians have no sense of time when it comes to appointments. It was a quarter to three when we reached his house. It is on a side street in an old residential quarter of town called the Arbat, a section in which the Vakhtangov itself is located, along with some of the better shops, some mansions of the tsarist period, and a number of foreign embassies.

The Vakhtangov Theatre has two large apartment houses reserved for its company, and all its members, save those women whose husbands are not part of the Vakhtangov, live in one of the two buildings. Since Simonov is Artistic Director, and a People's Artist of the U.S.S.R., his apartment is presumably one of the best. The car drove through an arch into a courtyard and stopped before an unkempt doorway. A small black-eyed boy was standing in it, waiting to greet us.

"My grandson," said Reuben Nikolayevich.

The boy looked like his grandfather, who is a small, compact Armenian; he shook hands cheerfully and dashed out into the courtyard. We proceeded up a flight of rather musty stairs to the second floor. One of the ever-present paradoxes of Moscow is the contrast between the marble façade on the street and the crumbling rear: what my mother used to call "a Queen Anne front and a Mary Anne back." The Vakhtangov apartment house is no exception.

The entrance door opened into a small vestibule where we hung up our coats and hats. Then Reuben Nikolayevich ushered me into his study, a medium-sized room filled with many oversized, handsome nineteenth-century mahogany pieces, including a large desk, a grand piano, a round table, a number of armchairs. The walls were lined with bookcases, sketches, a large oil portrait of Simonov, signed photographs, framed playbills, all in relaxed confusion. In an alcove was a bed covered with an Oriental spread. Two large windows looked out on leafless treetops.

Dinner had been prepared by Simonov's daughter-in-law, who soon came in to tell us it was ready. She is an attractive blonde in her late twenties, an actress at the Lenin Komsomol Theatre. Her husband, Yevgeny, is about thirty-five and already prematurely graying. He, like his son in the courtyard below, resembles his father. He has the same hook nose and dark bright eyes.

"My wife died several years ago," said the head of the family, "and I was lonely until the children moved in with me."

We entered a small dining room furnished with Empire pieces made of some honey-colored wood. The kitchen opened off this room. I presume there was a bathroom and a room for Yevgeny and his family beyond, but I was not invited to tour the apartment. The small round table at which we sat was laden with all sorts of *zakuski,* or hors d'oeuvres. There was fresh gray caviar, red caviar, herring salad, and hot boiled potatoes. There was also tomato-and-cucumber salad, olives, delicious black bread, slabs of sweet butter, and flaky home-made pirozhki—pastries filled with meat, rice, or cabbage. Vodka and white wine and cognac were provided. The main course was roast veal. Afterward, we had luscious white grapes and a Russian cheese much like roquefort.

Since all of us were theatre people, the conversation was stage talk. Simonov is proud of his son, who directed *An Irkutsk Story,* which is, of course, the Vakhtangov's current big hit. Yevgeny has also directed his own father in *Filumena Marturano,* and he is responsible for the excellent staging of *Three Short Tragedies* by Pushkin, a bill of one-act plays. There was talk of these, of past productions, of the future, of the father's impending trip to Paris, of my Phoenix Theatre. Quickly it was dusk, and, since I was going to a performance at seven-thirty, time to take my leave. Downstairs in the courtyard the dozing chauffeur roused himself, grandson Simonov waved from among his playmates, and I drove away.

In no other country would such a small family dinner be worth recording in this fashion; in the Soviet Union it seems to me that it is.

The following Sunday I had another invitation, this one to the country home of Grigory Alexandrov, the eminent motion-picture director, and his equally famous actress wife, Lyubov Orlova. Yuri Zavadski, Artistic Director of the Mossoviet Theatre, had arranged the occasion, for Orlova is one of the leading performers of his company.

Since I had accepted a dinner invitation for that evening, it was arranged we would drive out "to drink tea" in the late afternoon. About three-thirty, Zavadski picked me up. He was accompanied by Vera Maretskaya, the other leading actress of the Mossoviet, who is well-known in the Soviet Union because of her many roles in cinema. Yuri Osnos, the translator of Tennessee Williams' *Orpheus Descending*, which the Mossoviet was just about to put into rehearsal, was at the wheel of the small sedan. It was about forty-five minutes' drive through fields already dappled with the first light snow of autumn. A few miles past Peredelkino, the writers' community where Pasternak lived and lies buried, we turned off the main highway and up a one-lane road that led through birch-and-pine woods. "Gromyko's *dacha*," my companions said, pointing to a comfortable-looking house on the left. A hundred yards beyond, we turned in through some modest stone-and-brick gates.

Alexandrov, dressed in gray flannel slacks and a sport jacket, met us in the yard. Waiting at the door was his wife, her golden hair beautifully coiffed, her smartly simple black afternoon dress relieved by a single jeweled clip on her left shoulder. From the entrance hall, we passed into a large two-story living-dining room. The walls were of white plaster, the ceiling beams showed. At the windows hung draperies that looked like English hand-blocked linen. Armchairs and a deep sofa were slip-covered with the same linen print. A broad, covered terrace looked out on birch woods. ("We live mostly out on the terrace in summer," they said.) A natural wood staircase mounted from the living room to the upstairs bedrooms. Across one corner of the living room was an open fireplace with a birch-wood fire blazing in it.

"This can't be the Soviet Union," I was tempted to exclaim. I might have been in the English or American countryside, in Austria or Scandinavia, or indeed anywhere in the world where people of culture and means live simply but tastefully in the country.

"Won't you have a cocktail?" my host inquired. It was the first time I'd heard the word used by a Russian in Moscow. He produced a small shaker, ice, and, finally, a drink that looked and tasted rather like a daiquiri. Because I felt sure this had been planned to please the American guest, I could not decline. Later, when we sat down for "tea," Alexandrov's aged mother joined us, for it seems to be the Russian custom for the mother, if widowed, to live with a son and his family. As at Simonov's apartment, the large refectory table was laden with hors d'oeuvres and with bottles of exotic vodkas and cognac.

There was much laughter. Everyone, except me who can never remember the point, told jokes. We spoke mostly in English, for all these people have traveled abroad. After "tea" (a refreshment which was never served), we took a little walk, scuffing through the wet leaves, which the snow had not yet covered, and breathing pine-scented air. When it was time to leave, my host and hostess pressed mementos on me. "To remember your visit," they said, as though I should be likely to forget it.

Not all my social connections were with men and women at the top of the pack. There was Valodya, for instance, who decided shortly after we met in the foyer of the Children's Theatre, where he is an actor, that I should be taken under his wing, or at least I sized it up that way. At our first meeting, I had given him my hotel telephone number and extension, but I never expected he would use it, for rare indeed is the Russian who initiates contact with foreigners when it requires using a tapped telephone or the censored mail. However, the generation which has reached its majority since

Stalin's death impresses me as having less timidity than the previous ones (Valodya was only sixteen when Stalin died in 1953), and therefore I should not have been taken aback, two weeks later, when I heard his voice on the phone. He was apologizing for his silence and explaining that he had not called as he had promised because he had been making a movie on location in Odessa. Now he was back at his regular job and hoped we could meet.

Meet we did, probably half-a-dozen times, although on the few occasions that he came to the hotel he always brought someone with him, so that, I presume, it would not look to the always watchful hotel detectives as though he had private business of a counterrevolutionary nature to conduct. And I was never invited to his home or to meet his widowed mother, herself a retired actress of the Moscow Art Theatre.

Through Valodya I learned a lot about the younger members of the intelligentsia and the kind of life they lead. This was his first year out of the Shchukin School of the Vakhtangov Theatre, and he was still spiritually tied to it, even though he had joined the Central Children's Theatre. He spent several days a week at his alma mater, where he was directing a student production of *The Diary of Anne Frank* and designing the scenery as well. In addition to this project, he had to attend rehearsals at the Children's Theatre of plays already in the repertoire, to be fitted into their casts (for most plays in Moscow are double-, sometimes triple-cast). He also had rehearsals at the theatre of a new production, in which he was creating a role, and, too, he had to take part in approximately six performances every week.

And this was not all, for there was also, of course, the film he had been working in. Its shooting schedule was erratic; on occasion, it took him off at eight in the morning for a full or a half-day at the studio. And on top of all this he had a regular commitment to read to children in a kindergarten somewhere. Often, his working day lasted sixteen hours. What a difference between his active life and the undirected emptiness of most of my young American actor friends during their first year in the profession!

Over the one or two meals we had together—hurried ones because of his schedule even more than because of mine—Valodya told me of his ambitions. He wants to be a *régisseur* and he dreams of establishing his own theatre with some of his colleagues, mostly his classmates at the Shchukin School. The artistic line of this projected theatre is already clear in his mind: It will be neo-romanticism. "Not the romanticism of Schiller or Hugo," he says earnestly, "but a romanticism that is expressive of our time. We have had enough of realism; it grows flat. Our people love the romantic. So do I."

In preparation for the day when he can have his own theatre, Valodya is following a course that other bright young men have taken before him, for two of Moscow's most talented and promising *régisseurs*, both ten years older than he, also began their directorial careers in the Children's Theatre. Oleg Yefremov began there, like Valodya, as an actor straight out of theatre school, moved on to directing, and broke away to form the Sovremennik. Anatoly Efros started as a director at the Central Children's Theatre, after completing the *régisseur's* course at the State Institute of Theatre Arts, and he continues to stage many of that theatre's most imaginative productions. While Efros is not yet the managing director of a theatre of his own, he is invited to direct elsewhere, and is responsible, for instance, for several excellent productions at the Ermolova Theatre.

It is interesting that the Central Children's Theatre should be the breeding ground for tomorrow's leaders, as well as for tomorrow's audience. I am reminded of a comparable plan of Michel St. Denis, George Devine, and Glen Byam Shaw when they were at the head of the Old Vic School in London.

They planned to form a "Young Vic," a theatre for children, as a bridge over which the young artist would travel from the training period to mature responsibility. Valodya, it seemed to me, had made a wise decision in joining the Central Children's Theatre.

This youngest generation in the theatre, of which Valodya is a member, is an impressive lot. Not all of them play Hamlet on a major Moscow stage at twenty-three as Edward Martsevich has done, but many of them have the technical training to do so. All of them are enormously interested in anything they can learn about the world outside the Soviet Union. Wherever I came across them—individually, as in the case of Valodya and his friends, or collectively, as at rehearsals of the Sovremennik Theatre, in the classrooms of theatre schools, and at the lectures I delivered—I found my conviction strengthened that this upcoming generation in days to come might lead Russia into a new freedom, if the Kremlin would only allow it. They might see a time when, thanks to them, the word coexistence would acquire the same meaning on both sides of the Iron Curtain, when, indeed, the very Iron Curtain itself would be melted. I sensed the will; I wish I could point the way.

In America, where until only recently an interest in the stage, in ballet and the dance, or in music was called longhaired, and where the appellation of egghead still carries slight opprobrium, it may be hard to conceive of a country where the contributions of artists and writers and academicians are cherished and rewarded equally with the contributions of the leaders of science, industry, and government, where the arts are looked upon as of such importance that a Minister of Culture speaks for them in the Council of Ministers.

In America, we honor political heroes—Washington, Lin-

coln, Jefferson, Roosevelt—by naming streets and squares in
their memory; so do the Russians. But the Russians go us one
better, for they name their streets and squares for artists, too:
There is, of course, Stanislavski Street, and there are Moskvin
and Kachalov streets. Gorki Street is one of the city's principal thoroughfares; so is Chaikovski Boulevard. There are
Pushkin Square and Mayakovski Square. In America, such
public acknowledgment seems limited to the rather intra-
mural distinction of having a Broadway theatre, or the peri-
patetic one of having a Pullman car, named for you. I do seem
to recall once spending a night on the "Edwin Booth."

Soviet society's appreciation of the artist is, I believe, con-
nected with the remarkable Russian desire for "culture."
Nowhere have I seen people read as omnivorously as they
do in the Soviet Union; nowhere are the museums as crowded
at all hours by so many earnest viewers, who trail after the
ubiquitous guides. The desire has become a near-anxiety. One
of my American friends living in Moscow has learned to take
advantage of this anxiety. Her story lends added evidence of
its existence: When the Moscow street urchins become too
much for her, clamoring incessantly, as they do, for chewing
gum or fountain pens (the two seem equated in their minds,
and they are just as happy with a stick of Wrigley's Spear-
mint as with a Parker Duofold), she looks at them sternly and
says, *"Vuy nekulturny,"* which means, "You're uncultured."
At this unexpected but desperately serious accusation, the
abashed youngsters silently turn on their heels and flee.

Yet the emergence of a Soviet elite must not mislead one
into presuming that the Communist system is breaking down,
as many who scan the horizon for such portents will be
tempted to hope. It is simply that in what is presumably a
classless society, the superiority or uniqueness of one individual's contribution to the common welfare over that of
others has come to be acknowledged and rewarded; and the

large majority of his fellow citizens look upon this as right
and proper. The important thing from the Communist viewpoint is that no member of this elite is able to capitalize on
his position in terms of private ownership or the "exploitation" of others. The only Sol Hurok in the U.S.S.R. is the
government; the head of a publishing house or a newspaper
will never own its presses; he will never be able to pass on
what he has built up as a "family business" to his son. All
are servants of the state, and not a few of the elite are members of the Party. Thus the elite has a vested interest, so to
speak, in the status quo. To talk of their incomes in terms
of a certain number of rubles per month is futile, for the
ruble has no meaningful external value with which it may
be compared. If I say that a top artist may earn twenty-five
thousand rubles a month, the only way this sum becomes significant is by pointing out that the average wage for a manual
laborer is in the neighborhood of fifteen hundred rubles per
month, that a television set costs seventeen hundred and fifty
rubles, and that a Moskvich automobile is priced at twenty-
five thousand rubles.*

These figures still provide no proper basis for comparison
with our artists' incomes, because the Russian artist has no
need to save money to provide for the three essentials for
which Americans save: the education of one's children, medi-
cal protection for oneself and one's family, and a nest egg for
old age. The Soviet state takes care of all three. Furthermore,
since it is expected that all women will have some occupation
in addition to that of "housewife," the support of a spouse
is not one's responsibility. Taxes are low by Western standards. The Russian is in a position, therefore, to spend a far,
larger percentage of his income than are we. Actually, the
only problem he faces is to find things on which to spend it.

* Throughout this book, wages and prices are given in the 1960 value of the
ruble.

Consumer goods of all kinds are still scarce, despite the full
shop windows and the improvements in the quality as well as
the variety of clothing and foodstuffs. Foreign travel is possible only to a limited degree: Members of the intelligentsia
are almost the only Russians who may leave the country, and
they usually go in groups. There is a certain amount of inter-
course with the satellite countries, and a number of my Russian theatrical friends have been to Poland, to Romania,
and the other Eastern "republics"; but it is a far smaller number who have been to Paris, Vienna, London, or Rome (and
these only briefly), and an even tinier number who have been
to New York and Los Angeles. Furthermore, few of these trips
have been "just for fun." They have been part of cultural exchanges or specific missions; consequently, these artists can
be said to have been traveling only in the service of their
country. Opportunities to mingle with their opposite numbers, especially in the West, have been negligible.

A visitor's opinion of a country is apt to be determined less
by "sights" and scenery than by its inhabitants. So much depends on the kind of people whom one gets to know best.
I am really acquainted with only two kinds of Russians:
bureaucrats and artists. The former I have come into contact
with through the government or its various agencies, such as
Intourist. This type of person is more often than not humor-
less, condescending to the Westerner, unemotional, filled
with a sense of his own importance, noncommittal, severely
courteous. One imagines him—or her—to be personally am-
bitious, though for what goal, I'm not sure—power, probably,
for the greater the power, the greater the security. Because the
bureaucrats are associated in one's mind with that so-accurate
remark made by the Marquis de Custine in 1839, "Russia is the
land of useless formalities," one finds oneself at some point
or other in one's relations with them driven to extremes of

un-Christian irritation, which one regrets having exhibited as soon as the discovery is made that they almost seem to enjoy one's frustration. At the same time you learn that they can be bullied. At the personal level this type seems to react as the Russians do at the national level: They know the meaning of force, and if one exhibits more of it than they do, they will be apt to back down. In other words, because they represent what strikes me as the worst in Soviet society, they bring out the worst in the visitor. One reason, I suspect, why many tourists come away embittered from the Soviet Union is because their personal relations have been restricted to dealing with Soviet bureaucrats. I certainly do not know how the foreign press and the diplomatic and consular corps maintain aplomb, for their business forces them to deal almost exclusively with this type of citizen.

I am happy to say that the Russian artists seem to be as annoyed by their bureaucrats as I am. In these artists I find most of the opposite traits: a strong sense of humor that ranges from the sharp wit of the artist-*régisseur,* Nikolai Akimov, to the simple, spirited love of laughter all Russian artists possess; modesty; personal dignity; concern for the welfare of others. Always I was pushed onto a crowded bus ahead of my companion, male or female; more than once I was taken aside and asked by each of three different Russians whether I might not be in need of rubles which he offered to lend me.

In many countries, including our own, artists of the theatre are likely to be looked upon, and sometimes with some justification, as bohemians, with a looser standard of living than their fellows, with more unconventional modes of expression, behavior, and dress. This is not true in the Soviet Union. There, artists share the majority's strict sense of propriety. There is, indeed, almost an air of innocence about them.

They, like all Russians, are easily shocked, as much by exposure of the human body as by explicit use of four-letter words.
The world of Tennessee Williams is not for them; they
simply would not understand it. When they condemn the
West for its decadence, I don't think they really know what
they mean—or rather what the word means to us. I draw this
conclusion both from my observation of the people I know
and from the picture of their life as depicted on the stage.

It is not possible to say that sexual irregularities do not
exist, but I was struck by how many more very young Russian
people of the theatre are married than is so elsewhere. There
are both social and economic reasons for this. It is true that
in Russia, as almost nowhere else, two *can* live as cheaply as
one: Beyond the age of twenty-one, a single person is much
more heavily taxed than a married one, and, since both part-
ners of a marriage will have employment, their joint income
will be sizeable. Also, there is strong social pressure these
days for marriage: Witness the grand new "marriage palaces"
in many large cities, designed to make the ceremony and accompanying celebration as attractive as possible. I suspect,
too, that the present younger generation in the theatre, as
well as elsewhere, seeks an emotional stability which the generations immediately after the Revolution lacked and indeed
looked down upon as bourgeois.

No, Soviet performing artists do not strike me as bohemians
or as beatniks, but as industrious, conscientious, responsible
members of society, without flamboyance in dress, with an
almost old-world courtesy. (It is not unusual to see a young
as well as an old man bend over a woman's hand and kiss it
when greeting her.) It is, instead, the parochialism of the
Soviet artist that one regrets. This parochialism must be a
result of his isolation from the world community of thought
and taste. One runs into ignorance and misconceptions at
every turn, such as the manner in which the modern West-

ern world is presented on stage in clichés that bear slight resemblance to reality. If the Russian theatre is less good today than it has been and than it should be, it is perhaps necessary to look only at the fact that, generally speaking, its artists have been practically nowhere. Thus they really breathe no air but Russia's. The damage the Soviet theatre suffers from this isolationist policy of the government is irreparable.

11

"Home Thoughts
from Abroad"

At five minutes past eight on the evening of November 22, 1960, the Warsaw train pulled out of Moscow's Byelorusski Station exactly on time. The waving figures on the platform receded and disappeared. For the third time in my life I was leaving Moscow behind and, as twice before, I wondered to myself, "Shall I ever come here again?" The thought that perhaps I would not tinged the moment with regret. Then, as I looked out at the vanishing lights of the city, there came a knock on the door of my old-fashioned, mahogany-paneled compartment, and Igor Kvasha and Oleg Tabakov slid the door open. I had discovered that morning at a dress rehearsal of the Sovremennik Theatre that these two members of its acting company were going as far as Minsk on the same train as I; and, on the platform, I had run into them as they stood in the center of a little group under the clock. They were off for three or four days of location shooting for a movie in which they had small parts.

"We're going to the restaurant car and have something to eat," said Igor. "Won't you join us?"

A dining car on a Russian train is not exactly packed with old-world charm. The light is too cold and bright; the lone waitress is too tired, even at the beginning of the journey; the menu is too limited; the tablecloth too dirty. Still, it provides a place to sit and talk. We found a table for three, and I asked only for cheese and a glass of beer. The boys, however, were hungry, and each ordered a steak topped with a fried egg. On the table also appeared the omnipresent little glasses of vodka, with which we drank each other's health.

A couple of hours later, when it seemed time to head back to our compartments, young Igor, who is short, with dark hair and eyes, and the less shy of the two, said, "Now that you're leaving, what can you say about the way things have changed with us since you were here twenty-five years ago?"

His question was ill-timed. To answer it properly would have taken the rest of the night. Besides, my knowledge of Russian was too limited to explore the subject adequately, and neither young man spoke English. Furthermore, I had not yet had a chance to sort out my thoughts, and so I replied with a few banalities. Shortly thereafter, we, or rather they, paid the bill, and we pursued our rocky way back to my sleeping car, where they dropped me off at my door.

If we had sat up talking all night as the Moscow-Warsaw express swept westward across the vast Russian countryside, Igor might have heard some of the thoughts and reactions these pages have contained. Yet, I have not written this book to edify or instruct the Russians. In taking a sabbatical from my own Phoenix Theatre, I hoped to accomplish two goals: first, to bring myself up-to-date on what is happening in the Soviet theatre and, hopefully, to be reinvigorated; second, to acquire in the process some perspective on our own American theatre. Now that the trip is done and my observations of

Moscow's stages all but completely set down, I find that in many ways I was already up-to-date before I started. Many of the characteristics I note today, many of the conclusions I draw, are the same characteristics and conclusions I noted and drew twenty-five years ago. I have found less new territory to discover than I might wish. Nevertheless, out of the experience I draw certain reaffirmations. Such reaffirmations are good for the soul, and once every quarter-century they can perhaps be restated. Most of them arise from qualities that the Russian theatre possesses uniquely, qualities that have little to do with politics or social systems, although they perhaps have something to do with the essence of the people themselves.

In the first place, let me reaffirm my belief in knowing what one is doing in theatrical work. The Russians have thought about the creative process. They have analyzed means and methods. In consequence, they know what they want and, in most instances, how to achieve it on the stage. When an actor or a director in Moscow says he agrees with the Stanislavski system and with the principles of the MXAT up to a point, whereat he deviates, his statement is based on a conscious examination of methods and practices. Furthermore, this methodology is passed along to succeeding generations through the theatre schools. The youngsters at the Shchukin School know they are making preparations to extend the teachings of Vakhtangov. They know what he stood for; they are learning how to achieve the results he demanded. At the Art Theatre, the younger generation learns from the men—like Mikhail Kedrov—who learned the meaning of the Stanislavski system from the master himself. If they break away, as the Sovremennik group has done, they know why and what they want to do instead. There is constant self-examination, which is inculcated in the beginner from the start of his training and which continues throughout his life.

It is true that the American theatre has today acquired much more sophistication in its educational procedures than it possessed twenty-five years ago. We are deeply indebted to Lee Strasberg, to Elia Kazan, and to Cheryl Crawford for founding the Actors Studio, which emphasizes that training does not end with graduation from school, but is a process that mature actors need to continue if their work is to remain fresh. If anything, we have gone to excess, it seems to me, in this matter of training. Almost every young actor and every would-be actor in New York goes to "classes." It is the thing to do, and it often does not seem to matter from *whom* he learns or *what* he learns. Yet, while this is certainly better than the reverse situation, I fear there is today too much indiscriminate utilization of the "class" as a substitute for the real thing. For this state of affairs I blame the young actors less than our system, or rather, our lack of system. Most young actors would far rather work in a play than go to class. Since, however, there are so few jobs and since unemployment is the rule rather than the exception in our theatre, classwork provides compensating exercise, even though too often it becomes preparation for work that never comes.

But do all these classes and all this study result in a real knowledge of what we are doing? (I except, of course the study of such specific techniques as voice, diction, body movement, dance, fencing.) I have yet to hear an American actor who believes in "the Method" tell me precisely what he means by the phrase; I have yet to hear an American actor who has no faith in it tell me explicitly what he practices instead, what he depends upon as "technical means for the creation of the creative mood," as Stanislavski put it; I have yet to read any prominent American director's statement of his artistic credo that could lead me to an understanding of precisely what it is for which he stands. The American theatre has still found no satisfactory substitute for the intuitive process. Things are still hit-or-miss.

In the second place, let me reaffirm the value I place on the Russian theatre's sense of relationship to the past. It seems strange that I find this sense stronger in the land of revolution, in the Union of Soviet Socialist Republics, than in the more conservative United States of America. But I do. In the United States, the masterpieces of the past are works of art to be studied in school and then discarded, like a knowledge of Latin which doesn't help much when shopping at Macy's. The great heritage of dramatic literature which is shared by the entire world is heedlessly tossed aside by Americans, both artists and public. What, they ask, have Sophocles or Molière, Ben Jonson or Calderón, Ibsen or Gogol to say to us?

In the Soviet Union, however, the classics are devoured avidly; Pushkin, Lermontov, and Tolstoi are read and re-read, recited aloud, constantly performed. During October, 1960, before the season was yet in full swing, there were forty plays presented in Moscow that antedated the Revolution. Broadway in that same month offered not a single play written before 1917. Indeed, during the entire preceding season, the American commercial theatre had originated but three revivals of great works by past masters, *Much Ado About Nothing, Heartbreak House,* and an evening entitled *Dear Liar,* which was based on the Shaw-Campbell letters and which was not strictly a drama. Throughout the 1958–1959 Broadway season, only one revival was offered: Sean O'Casey's *The Shadow of a Gunman.*

Our aversion to the theatrical past does not obtain in the other arts. Last year, more people visited New York City's

Metropolitan Museum of Art, the great repository of past masterpieces, than visited the Museum of Modern Art and the Solomon R. Guggenheim Museum combined. The New York Philharmonic Symphony society would no more think of banishing from its repertoire Bach, Beethoven, Brahms, and all composers who wrote before 1917 than the Metropolitan Opera would think of discarding the works of Mozart, Verdi, Wagner, and all the other eighteenth- and nineteenth-century composers. The public would not stand for it. Our great heritage in music, painting, and sculpture we treasure. We have no use for the past in drama.

The Phoenix Theatre, of which I can speak with authority, has presented in eight seasons twenty-two works antedating 1917; only three have received sufficient public support to pay back the cost of mounting them. As a result of this lack of demand for the recreated works of the past on the part of the public, there has inevitably grown up a generation of artists who would not know how to interpret these works if popular interest did suddenly revive in them. The demands upon directors and actors which Marlowe, Molière, or Maeterlinck impose are severe. The tough realism that American actors know how to command stands them in no stead when faced with *Edward the Second* or *Tartuffe* or *The Death of Tintagiles.* But since they have little likelihood of ever being called upon to perform these works, why prepare themselves? The result is that American actors are as limited in their command of styles as Russian actors are versatile. This is a great loss, for a familiarity with truly great works of genius both enriches the interpreter and gives him humility. Our actors have nothing whatever to be proud of, simply because they can do a creditable job of impersonating the familiar but superficial characters invented by William Inge, Paul Osborn, or Samuel Taylor, to mention some of our best contemporary playwrights.

A sense of a truly working relationship with the past is essential for the artist of today, if he is to maintain a perspective on his own life and times. The Russians, who have broken with their past more completely than any other people in the world, have returned to it forty years after the break, not with the thought of reproducing it, but of reinterpreting it so as to give added meaning to the present day. Our reinterpretations would doubtless not be the same as theirs, but at least let us have some ideas of our own. I find it difficult to understand why so few of the most talented directors in the American theatre ever attempt to reinterpret for our time any masterpiece from the history of the world's great dramatic literature.

In the third place, let me reaffirm my belief in the dignity of the artist in the theatre. I regret that I have to go back to Moscow to recover this. Again, it is our system, not the individual, that is to blame. Our commercial theatre looks upon artists as a product to be bought and sold. In time, the artist looks upon himself in the same way. The actor, and to a lesser extent the director, the playwright, and even the producer, is thrust by the exigencies of our commercialism into a dog-eat-dog competitive arena. Much of the time his fate—which is to say, his artistic career—is in the hands of some middleman, some agent who "represents" him, who will work out "package deals," determine where and under what circumstances he will work. In many instances, the good of the client is determined by what is good for the agent. I cannot think that, practical as this system may be, it is particularly ennobling. Nor do I think the theatre is healthier as a whole because of it.

In this competition, the objective is "success": a "hit" for the dramatist, to be associated with a "hit" for all the others. What does a hit actually mean? Simply that the thousands of dollars that were spent in bringing the play to life can be repaid to the investors out of box-office receipts, together with a profit left over for its backers and producer to share. When this occurs, it is the result, of course, of the fact that a very large number of people have been attracted to the play. Sometimes excellence is a contributing factor to this happy state of affairs, but not always. Sometimes it has been accomplished by a flair for promotion, such as is possessed by David Merrick; sometimes it results from the presence of a collection of "big names," as in the Rodgers-Hammerstein-Lindsay-Crouse-Mary Martin team that assured the "success" of *The Sound of Music* before it ever opened. Success and excellence are rarely to be equated in the American theatrical scheme of things. It is comforting to point to the number one long-running drama *Life with Father,* and say it deserved its success, but few honest critics, including its authors, would say it is the greatest play the American stage has ever produced, or that *Abie's Irish Rose* and *Tobacco Road,* the long-run runners-up, were the two other finest dramas of our theatrical century.

All this applies to actors and directors as well as to playwrights. The successful actor is he who most quickly or most constantly sees his name in Broadway lights and his signature on a movie or television contract. For the lights and the contracts mean money, and in the theatre, as elsewhere in American society, money spells success. But once again, success and excellence are not necessarily equated. Some of our most consummate artists are known and respected by but a fraction of the huge public that acclaims the "successful" personality.

Things are different in Moscow. A long time ago I concluded that for my Russian colleagues, "acting is an art to which they have dedicated themselves for its own sake and for the service of the people. In New York, an actor regu-

larly talks about his 'job.' I have never heard an actor in
Moscow so refer to his occupation, for he does not regard it
in this way. . . . The artists of Moscow are not jesters to
the public; they are its leaders, its teachers, its servants; they
are Russia's respected citizens, its great men."

What can be done to acquire for our theatre workers the
same sense of dignity, the same desire for service, the same
dedication to their art? Certainly, such a goal requires no
political alterations. I doubt that it requires social adjustments. It simply requires a recognition on the part of theatre
people themselves, accompanied by a recognition on the part
of the public, that theirs is a high calling. Yet this is easier
said than done. Indeed, it may never be done, as long as the
pressures of commercial exploitation of the theatre continue,
for commercialism is at the heart of the problem. But I am
not entirely convinced that this kind of exploitation is here
to stay. Broadway's plight had become so severe by the summer of 1961 that the New York *Times* published five ex-
haustive studies of its economic deterioration, in an effort,
presumably, to rally public support to force the commercial
theatre to clean its own house. The first season I was in the
Soviet Union, the season of 1934–1935, there were one hundred and forty-nine productions on Broadway; in 1960–1961,
there were forty-six. But in 1960–1961, there were ninety-five
productions presented off-Broadway. Very little of this off-
Broadway activity is commercially motivated. Naturally, the
off-Broadway manager would like to have a "hit," but his
choice of material has been dictated less by a search for what
the public wants than by a desire to give a hearing to something he feels has intrinsic merit. Excellence rather than success; recognition of such a motive is the first step toward a
reassertion of dignity and service.

With T. Edward Hambleton I founded the Phoenix

Theatre, geographically off-Broadway. Our first policy statement in 1953 indicated that we sought to create a theatre
where artists could work "free from the pressures of the hit-
or-flop pattern of Broadway." In the ensuing eight years, our
challenge has been met by over seven hundred actors, singers,
and dancers, who came to work at the Phoenix in our plays
and musicals. Some—Franchot Tone, Erich Leinsdorf, Paul
Draper, Geraldine Page, Cornelia Otis Skinner, Angna Enters
—came only for one night and for practically no compensa-
tion whatever. Others came for a period of weeks, but again
for a bare subsistence salary: Hollywood stars Montgomery
Clift, Farley Granger, Viveca Lindfors, and Robert Ryan,
for example; such European celebrities as actresses Irene
Worth, Joan Plowright, Siobhan McKenna; as well as directors Michael Redgrave, Tony Richardson, and Tyrone
Guthrie; Broadway stars of the senior generation like Lillian
Gish, Florence Reed, Blanche Yurka, and Eva Le Gallienne;
and such a host of other established actors that space forbids
listing even the better-known names. Some of the finest
American designers accepted both the budgetary limitations
of the Phoenix and a minimum fee for working there: Don-
ald Oenslager, Howard Bay, Boris Aronson, William and
Jean Eckart, and Will Steven Armstrong.

I offer this roster of names as evidence that artists of the
theatre do stand ready to serve, if the demand is made. And I
aver with confidence that all of these artists captured a new
sense of the worth and dignity of their profession by being
released—even temporarily—"from the pressures of the hit-
or-flop pattern." Only twice before has anything comparable
happened in our theatre in the last forty years: Eva Le Gallienne's Civic Repertory Theatre in the twenties, and the
Group Theatre in the thirties. Those were also moments of
dedication and service.

There are other theatrical projects in existence or im-
minent that quicken my hope for a new day of dignity and
worth in the American theatre. With dedication and courage
and a conviction that the stage is more than a commercial
enterprise, Arena Stage sprang up in Washington, the Alley
Players in Houston, the Actors' Workshop in San Francisco
—all professional enterprises. They followed in the wake of
the late Margo Jones's project in Dallas and of semi-profes-
sional, noncommercial theatres like the Cleveland Play House
and the Pasadena Playhouse, which for decades have maintained high artistic standards outside of New York. In Minneapolis, a resident professional theatre, led by Tyrone
Guthrie and Oliver Rea, is on the way to becoming a reality:
More than one million dollars has been pledged to provide
the Twin Cities, Minneapolis and St. Paul, with a theatre
worthy of their excellent symphony orchestra and their
Walker Art Gallery.

To contradict, in part, my generalization that the American public has no use for the classics, the American Shakespeare Festival Theatre has been established during the last
decade in Stratford, Connecticut, and it has become "successful"; other Shakespearean festivals have been conducted
at Ashland, Oregon, San Diego, California, Yellow Springs,
Ohio, and elsewhere. The most spectacular and potentially
the most influential project in creating a new climate for
drama is the Lincoln Center for the Performing Arts. This
dream of John D. Rockefeller III and his associates demands
not only millions of dollars for its realization, but also a
body of artistic talent that can create a truly great repertory
theatre. The challenge is the greatest our theatre has yet
faced, and the opportunity is the greatest. If it establishes
excellence rather than success as its criterion in selecting
plays and players, it can go a long way by the force of its
example toward a new orientation on the part of the public

and artists necessary, I believe, if we are to meet the Russians on their own high level of dedication in art.

In the fourth place, let me reaffirm my belief in collective endeavor in the theatre. I have been asserting this article of faith for as long as I have been in the theatre. I have yet to see it become a living reality in America, and, for deeply psychological reasons, I may never see it realized here. But that need not prevent me from voicing it once again.

My first experience in the professional theatre was as a member of a collective called the University Players. My association with it began early in the 1930's, and we were all of an age—about a decade younger than the century. Starting as a summer company, before some of our number had yet graduated from college, a nucleus of about a dozen of us persevered for five years, even through a cataclysmic attempt to play in true repertory in Baltimore one winter. In addition to the dozen members were others who stayed for awhile and moved on—about eighty, all told. The group was led by Charles Leatherbee, Joshua Logan, and Bretaigne Windust; it included Henry Fonda, Margaret Sullavan, James Stewart, Kent Smith, Myron McCormick, Mildred Natwick, and Barbara O'Neil.

We came together almost by chance; we stayed together because we found it personally rewarding to be part of an ensemble, to merge our individual talents in a collective enterprise. The dream which "Charlie, Windy, and Josh" held out to us was of a theatre like the Moscow Art Theatre, where Leatherbee and Logan had spent some weeks in 1931 and had come under the personal spell of Stanislavski. The dream never materialized, but not because it was invalid.

Unquestionably, this initial experience made a profound impression on me. It was strengthened three years later by my own first exposure to the Soviet theatre, whose per-

manently organized collectives seemed to me to be in large
measure responsible for what I found there that was good.
The almost tangible oneness that a sensitive visitor feels as
he walks backstage in a Moscow theatre—in the wings, in
the greenroom, in the offices, in rehearsal halls; the fraternity
that exists there and which extends from older actors to
young ones, to stage mechanics, to elderly stage doormen—
is totally unfamiliar to him, if he has been brought up on
Broadway or on London's Shaftesbury Avenue. There, it is
every man for himself. Competition is the lifeblood. In seeking the reason for this contrast, one is drawn into an examination of one of the fundamental dissimilarities between
the Russians and ourselves: their spirit of community versus
our spirit of individualism.

This Russian communal sense can be traced back to peasant and ecclesiastical origins. We all know that the Western
ideal of democracy is based on sacred respect for the individual; we all know how the spirit of Protestantism, which
our first settlers brought to New England, sprang only in
part from revolt against the English crown and that, more
profoundly, it began with the Reformation and had deeply
religious as well as deeply political implications. We know
less well the Greek Orthodox church and its effect on the
Eastern European mind and spirit. In Greek Orthodox
teachings, the way to God is not a solitary path, but one
trod jointly with the rest of the Lord's children. When the
Bolsheviks overthrew the church along with the government,
they sought to replace the former with a new orthodoxy, yet
still with a belief making much the same basic appeal: one
for all—the submersion of self in a communal experience.
"The consciousness of personality," writes George Fedotov
in *The Russian Religious Mind,* "of its own ways, vocations,
and rights developed tardily and slowly on the Russian soil
both in pagan and in Christian times. This is the deepest

religious root of Russian collectivism." This submersion was a familiar part of Russian life long before the Revolution. The peasants lived communally. Even their relationship to the landowners acknowledged the communal basis. *Dr. Zhivago* is full of this. So are the plays of Chekhov and the novels of Turgenev and Tolstoi and Dostoyevski. For the fact is, as Wright Miller points out in *Russians as People,* "that while Russian history has been strong in forces tending to preserve the traditional collective life, it has always been weak in forces which could develop the status and rights of the individual."

One of the first things that strikes one about the Russians is their use of each other's first names and patronymics immediately upon being introduced. The reason I find this significant is that it seems to strengthen a fraternal bond which cuts across artificial barriers. No porter, no student actor at the Moscow Art Theatre would ever have thought of addressing their great and highly revered master, Stanislavski, as anything other than Constantin Sergeyevich, just as he in turn would address them by their first names and patronymics. This ancient custom has nothing to do with tsarism or with communism. It is, instead, deeply a part of the Russian relationship of man to man. It expresses a Russian's sense of fraternity. It is a badge of his membership in the communal family.

It is this lack of the highly developed Western sense of separateness, I suppose, that permits the Russian to endure the inconvenience of sharing living quarters with virtual strangers; that allows him to find nothing odd in four persons, of either sex, sharing one sleeping compartment on a railroad train; that causes him to accept, as the day's pattern, eating, working, studying, and playing jointly with other members of his "collective." Applied to the theatre, it explains why the whole organization of the Russian stage is

basically so different from ours. It explains why there are no
"stars" on Moscow's stages, whereas Broadway can scarcely
subsist without them. It explains why the ensemble is so
much more important to the Russian stage than is the individual; why the relationship between audience and performers has a solidarity in Russia beyond that which it possesses
in other countries; why a Russian feels fulfilled in a theatre
where he may play the lead tonight and walk-on bits for the
next three nights, and still plan to be a member of that one
collective enterprise throughout his performing life; and
why, conversely, the American theatre may never altogether
lose the individualism that is both its curse and its strength.

When the Phoenix Theatre seemed unable to acquire a
face of its own three or four years after its founding, I accepted the judgment of Tyrone Guthrie and others that perhaps it would never do so until it represented a collective
enterprise. The effort to bring a permanent acting company
into being took T. Edward Hambleton and me another three
years, for nothing in the American theatre is more difficult—
financially and psychologically—than to establish a "repertory company." We hear enthusiastic lip service widely paid
to the concept. But the actor in New York shrewdly counters,
when faced with a firm offer to join a permanent company,
"What's in it for me? What parts shall I play? If I get a
better offer, can I withdraw?"

I sympathize with this caution. I understand it. But I
know that no Russian actor asks these questions. For this inviolability of the individual, to give it a grand name, is a
Western concept. It underlies our entire way of life. Indeed,
it is what we have fought in time past to defend, and would
fight again to preserve. On the other hand, collectivism has,
at once, everything to do with communism and nothing to
do with it.

We may well be as unable to accept the concept of collectivism in the arts as we would be unable to accept it in politics. Both are very close to the Russians and very far from us. Yet, notwithstanding, I keep returning to the idea of a "collective" theatre. And I do so because I have seen better work done by ensembles than by hastily and temporarily assembled troupes: by such ensembles as the Moscow Art Theatre and other Russian companies, by the Abbey Theatre, by the Théâtre National Populaire, by the Group Theatre. I do so because the very nature of theatrical expression dictates a joint undertaking. A play is fashioned out of human beings interacting upon one another. A performance brings this interaction to life, and the more completely realized the interaction, the more satisfactory the end result. No play can be produced without people working together. Therefore, why not create circumstances under which this coöperation can be fully utilized? I believed a permanent, or at least semi-permanent, collective is the only way.

To my gratification, I see today powerful forces being exerted to make this dream come true in America. The Ford Foundation in 1959 announced grants totaling more than half-a-million dollars to four theatres, one each in New York, Washington, Houston, and San Francisco, to be used to establish resident companies. The over eight-million dollar dramatic theatre unit of the Lincoln Center for the Performing Arts is being erected for the announced purpose of housing a "repertory company." Possibly, just possibly, it pays to keep stating a credo over and over again. We shall see.

The first four reaffirmations I have expressed above after my return from Moscow—a belief in knowing what you are doing, in having a sense of relationship to the past, in the dignity of the artist in the theatre, and in collective endeavor —concern things which the Russians, I feel, are realizing better than, at least at this time of writing, Americans are. I have a fifth reaffirmation, however, to which the Russians cannot subscribe and which quite possibly makes the balance: I wish to reaffirm a belief in freedom of expression. The trip to Moscow brings home, in no uncertain terms, the essentialness of freedom. The lack of it is the principal reason why the Soviet theatre is no better than it was a quarter-century ago. The barren plateau on which the theatre stood for almost twenty years, after its breath-taking ascent during the preceding two decades, was a wasteland brought into being because freedom of expression was snatched away from the Russian theatre.

If Meierhold had been allowed to bring his life's work to final fulfillment; if those disciples who wanted to carry it forward had been allowed to do so; if other artists had felt free to choose their own creative lines, whether they led toward socialist realism or away from it; if playwrights could have written whatever their perception of man compelled them to write, whatever their imaginations dictated; the Soviet theatre might still be the best in the world. But the government and the Party saw fit to impose their own demands, on pain of exile or death or silence. Artists cannot create in an aura of fear, whether it be induced by McCarthyism in America or by communism in Russia. Fortunately, our freedom was tampered with for only a few years; in Moscow it disappeared for a generation, and, in fact, the Russians have never possessed freedom in its fullest form.

To say that Soviet freedom of expression has returned is, of course, inaccurate. There is only relatively more freedom than there was in the last decades under Stalin. Whether this trend continues to increase will depend on two things: on whether or not it is abused by headstrong and irresponsible writers and creative artists, and on the rate of the Communist Party's growth of self-confidence. I am not sanguine over the outcome. Yet, before we become too smug over our own use of freedom, it behooves us to take a realistic look at ourselves. In the question period that followed the lecture I gave at the Polytechnical Museum in Moscow, three separate slips of paper were passed up to the podium asking, "Is there censorship of the theatre in the U.S.A.?" My answer, of course, was, "No—save of the obscene and the pornographic." It would have been too tricky to try to qualify my answer further. But qualified it should have been. For, while our government exercises at no level the kind of censorship my Soviet interrogators had in mind, it is nevertheless true that freedom of expression knows certain bounds. It is only as absolute as is man's freedom to starve. Political censorship has been replaced by economic and social censorship, exercised not by the government but by the public.

This, I suppose, is as it should be in a working democracy. The voice of the people—public opinion—dictates. But who controls public opinion? Madison Avenue? The dramatic critics of the newspapers? Current fads and fetishes? The financial interests behind the television networks and the motion-picture companies? Certainly, I am free to write what I please in America, but I am not free to get it produced, unless I have the money myself. Certainly, I am free to announce any play I choose for production in my theatre, but if my choice is vetoed too many times by the press, acting as arbiters of public taste, I shall go bankrupt. Perhaps true freedom of expression exists nowhere in the theatre. We are, no doubt, a hundred times better off than the Russians; but often I think that thought control, subtly exercised, is almost as dangerous to our democracy as is the blatant and forceful repression of the totalitarian states. Our lives may not be in danger. But what about our spirits?

This is not the point at which I want to leave either the Soviet or the American theatres. I am by nature an optimist, and I refuse to write finis to this book with words so gloomy. Let me, therefore, offer a final reaffirmation, one of faith in the theatre itself and in its certainty of survival. To date, the greatest days of the Soviet theatre have been those which took place during the agonizing early years of the Revolution. That the vigorous Moscow theatre of the years 1917–1927 could have withstood such fire and tempest is vivid testimony to its rugged disposition. That the theatre subsequently survived purges and blackouts of its freedom, and that it looks toward the future with the confidence I felt and heard on every side in Moscow in 1960, persuades me that the theatre in Russia is still, indeed, a rugged institution. Ten years from now, the Soviet theatre may well be leading the world once again. It has solid foundation stones on which to build. It has idealists with the knowledge and the dedication to lift it high.

Our American theatre, it is true, has had no such trial by fire, and perhaps this is why it seems relatively weaker. But it has undergone tribulations of other sorts. It has faced the assault of the mass media—of motion pictures, of radio, and of television—to an extent that the Soviet theatre has not yet begun to experience. It has retrenched and regrouped its forces. It is perhaps today close to rock bottom, economically speaking. But during the very years when the Russians were standing still, during this last quarter-century, we have seen great things in American theatre. We have seen what could happen when the government took the unprecedented step of creating a Federal Theatre Project back in the 1930's. The government may have jumped in for the wrong reason and jumped out again for the wrong reason, but it stayed there long enough to write a glorious chapter in the history of our modern stage. We have seen magnificent theatres built on the campuses of great American universities—buildings equipped with the best that state or private funds and individual imaginations could supply, and surpassing the best playhouses of the Soviet Union. Out of these buildings, and a hundred more modest plants, comes the generation that will create and will support tomorrow's stage. We have seen one hundred million dollars raised by private enterprise, not by government levy, to erect a great center for the performing arts in the greatest city in the world. We have seen in that same city more than thirty tiny stages rise up to challenge the monopoly of Broadway, as young people undertook by themselves to remedy some of the ills of the commercial theatre of which they and the general public had too long been the victims. We have seen, in twenty-five years, Eugene O'Neill bring his career to a triumphant close. We have discovered Thornton Wilder and William Saroyan and Lillian Hellman and, later, Tennessee Williams and Arthur Miller, a quintet of playwrights whose joint output exhibits a variety and power which the Russians cannot possibly match. If ten years from now the Soviet theatre does indeed lead the world once again, I pray that the American theatre will give it a run for its money. I know that it can. I believe that it will.

Index

Index